OUR
GENEROUS
GENE

OUR GENEROUS GENE

Mike Dickson

THE GENEROUS PRESS

First published in Great Britain in 2015 by
The Generous Press, 28 Portobello Road, London W11 3DH

This edition published 2015
© Michael Dickson 2015
mike@rainmakerfoundation.org
www.rainmakerfoundation.org
www.ourgenerousgene.com

Printed in Great Britain by Clays Ltd, St Ives plc
Cover design: ArtBiro Network
Typesetting: Ed Pickford

ISBN: 978-0-9551591-3-8

To Shuna – my wonderful wife.
The most remarkable, loving, generous and
patient woman I know.

Thank you

It wouldn't have been possible to write this book without the input and encouragement of a wonderful group of people who offered introductions, told me their stories, read the draft and were unfailingly supportive and generous with their time.

Annabel Dickson; Andy Blackford; Adrian Bethune; Charles Handy; Claire Allen; 'Dan' and his team; David Gold; Doug Scott; Ellie Besley Gould; Fred FitzGerald; Jessica Barratt; John Davy; John Sweeney; Julia Lalla-Maharajh; Reverend Mark Hargreaves; Mark Williamson; Michael Norton; Olly Donelly; Orly Wahba; Pam Warhurst; Pete Yeo; Shuna; Steve Spall; Susannah Steele; Terry Pulling; Thiywe Khumalo; Tristram Stuart; Dr Vincent Pattison; Wendy Tracey; William Dickson.

Thank you all for being such stars!

Contents

The More You Give, The More You Get

The more you give, the more you get.
The more you laugh, the less you fret.
The more you do unselfishly,
The more you live abundantly.
The more of everything you share,
The more you'll always have to spare.
The more you love, the more you'll find
That life is good and friends are kind.
For only what we give away,
Enriches us from day to day.

Helen Steiner Rice

Introduction

Surprised by Life

Life's a challenge – grab it!

P ut the clock back to 1989. I'm being asked: 'So what's someone your age [forty-two] and your size [a 'non-athletic' build] doing running a marathon?'

Getting myself round the London Marathon – in about three times the time it takes the elite athletes – did make me fitter, but it wasn't the run that changed my life; it was deciding that there had to be a point to it.

Some years before, a young girl in a powered wheelchair had driven into the shop I owned in London's Covent Garden. She pressed a control and her seat rose to the same height as the counter. She paid, lowered the seat and then sped out into the piazza. I remember thinking at the time that it must surely be an expensive piece of kit, and I was intrigued and impressed enough to have remembered the name of the manufacturer.

With just weeks to go before the marathon, I got in touch with them. The wheelchairs cost £3,500 each and there was a waiting list of over 100 children, who all wanted one but couldn't afford it. The company suggested I meet a young girl called Sammy, who had cerebral palsy and lived with her grandmother in Lincoln. As much to give myself courage and inspiration for the marathon ahead as anything else, I cleared a day and went to Lincoln.

Sammy and her grandmother greeted me at the station and took me home to tea. I had never met a disabled child before and had no idea what cerebral palsy was. After spending just two hours in Sammy's company, I was both profoundly moved and motivated. Sammy was bright, but had trouble with her speech and very limited movement, making her reliant on friends and her grandma, who had to push Sammy's very basic wheelchair if she wanted to get out and about. I left with a photo of Sammy and, together with my running partner, Ricky, we wrote begging letters to everyone we could think of: 'We are going to do something daft and mildly heroic; run 26.2 miles to help a young girl who can't move about independently to get out of her front door on her own.'

By the day of the London Marathon, neither of us had run more than six miles in training, but we had raised over £9,000, an extraordinary sum in those days. There was a brief discussion before the start: 'Even if we don't finish, we can't let Sammy down, we need to get her that wheelchair!'

Six hours and thirty minutes later, when all the traffic-separation schemes had been removed, I staggered across the finishing line. Ricky had made it in a more respectable five hours.

Mission accomplished! But, looking back, our mission had only just started. As the money came in, questions were being asked: 'There must be lots of children like Sammy needing wheelchairs. Are there charities to help them?' We checked, and we met with the major disability charities (initially thinking, *surely there were enough charities already?*), but they confirmed there was a gap to fill. Out of the blue, a friend with charity experience (we had none) offered to jump through the necessary hoops to register a new charity; another friend, without even being asked, offered seed funding to help us get started. Nine of us ran the New York Marathon that autumn, raising £45,000, and in April 1990, just a year after Ricky and I had made it round London, Whizz-Kidz was registered as a charity.

In 2015, Whizz-Kidz celebrated its twenty-fifth anniversary. It has become the largest supplier of paediatric mobility aids across the UK outside the NHS and has raised over £100 million. Over 20,000 young people are whizzing about their lives more confidently because it's been there for them. Arunima (who got her first Whizz-Kidz wheels when she was fourteen, followed by another at eighteen to equip her for Cambridge Uni) attended the anniversary celebrations. She's twenty-eight now, and a lawyer. I also met up again with Ruth at the party. She had her first Whizz-Kidz chair when she was five and is now working in the fundraising team. A whole generation of wheelchair-users have become Whizz-Kidz ambassadors. Never in my wildest dreams could I have predicted the impact it would have on so many people's lives – least of all mine.

Sammy's new wheelchair may have helped make Sammy's life a little bit better – but it completely changed mine. I discovered a great deal about how charities work, and gradually awakened from my own small, self-centred world. I started to experience the positive impact of giving. I noticed that, more often than not, when a fundraiser met a disabled young person – often the child for whom they had raised money – it had an enormous positive impact, way beyond the simple understanding of the difference mobility would make to that child's self-confidence and independence to get to school or go shopping on their own. Bankers, advertising execs, high-earners, nurses, teachers and cabbies: everyone shared in common the feeling that their relatively small fundraising efforts had been the best thing they had done all year. They were both amazed and humbled.

I discovered what an enormous privilege it is to be able to help others and how hugely rewarding it is to be able to inspire someone else to do likewise, because it makes for a happier and more fulfilling life. I was hugely lucky to be in the right place at the right time to help set up a charity for disabled children from a base of zero knowledge. It certainly hadn't been part of my personal life plan. But having benefited from that luck, I now had another responsibility. How could I spread the word about the amazing power of giving?

I decided to put my thoughts into a book of experiences and anecdotes. I hoped it would serve as a simple recipe for how anyone could make the world a better place and become happier and more fulfilled as they did so.

It was a small book – but it has made a difference. *Please Take One Step* was launched at TEDGlobal in 2010. As an ever-widening circle of people read it, they started emailing and calling me, wanting to participate in a more generous world, and from this swell of interest and willingness to help, the Rainmaker Foundation was born: a community of people committed to creating a world where what matters most is what we do for others.

And as Rainmakers act to make the world a better place, I am also encouraged by what's going on elsewhere. Much has changed since 2010 when I first put my thoughts on paper. Most of today's biggest online campaigners didn't exist before 2000 and many were small, even in 2010. When millions of people join, support and act to address injustices, they're simply taking a little bit of time to be generous. There are ever more movements of generous people doing generous things, sticking up for causes they care about or crowd-funding a total stranger's medical treatment because they can. There is global impetus creating positive change, often locally and experimentally; always collaboratively; initiatives that are 'biting off a bit of the elephant'; tackling some of the issues previously sidelined as just too big.

We can all make a choice to look for the good or bad in everything, and that choice will shape our future world. I believe we all have a Generous Gene – perhaps thousands of them – as part of our make-up, and in researching this book I've found academics, people whose life's work has been focused on understanding well-being and happiness, agree. I'm incredibly lucky to live a life where, by total serendipity, I see it at work. In our search for happiness and meaning, what I have learnt is that the good you do – however small and insignificant it may seem at the time – ripples outwards and has much more impact than you think; that positive action acts like a magnet for people to gather round. Groups of ordinary people can, and often do, change things for the better in a way that seems much more efficient and effective than the processes followed by those we elect. I've been privileged to meet many 'ordinary' people and spent many happy hours listening to their stories, some of which I've shared here.

My main reason for including a little of my own story is to encourage everyone to go for it. If a totally unathletic forty-two-year-old with no running experience – not much experience of any form of exercise, in fact – can survive a marathon, then start a disability charity without any knowledge of charities or disability and end up running a global foundation, then anyone can make a difference. I am amazed and surprised by life. Frankly, if I can do it, there is hope for everyone!

Mike Dickson
October 2015

Part 1

1

Growing Your Generous Gene

'Never believe that a few caring people can't change the
world. For, indeed, that's all who ever have.'

Margaret Mead, anthropologist

We're at a pivotal moment in history. You can feel it in the air, from casual conversations to global summits and mass protests. Most people in the world can communicate, collaborate, spread ideas and implement them at a rate our established systems struggle to cope with and adapt to.

The Information Age has changed us: the way we do business, the choices we make, the speed of that change. Of course, this cuts both ways: education, connection and enlightenment go hand in hand with images of violence and 37 million email addresses hacked from the Ashley Madison 'Life is short. Have an affair' website. I could go on but hopefully the point is made.

It's about choice. After more than a century of profit-driven capitalism, the unsettling thought we cannot ignore is that mines dug, profits earned and carbon emissions generated in remote corners of the world impact you and me. Blinkers off. Infinite economic growth – the mantra that unites economists, governments and profit-driven industries – isn't the way forward. There are plenty of reasons to be glum, but also to take this as a wake-up call to create the change we wish to see – a world where we're less stressed out and insecure about our future; where we focus more on creating a life worth living than on wealth and financial security. At that stage, our core values will have shifted away from *me*, *my* country, *my* profit and *my* self-interest to a realisation that our world is a better place when we nurture and share what we have between us. And the amazing thing is that when we focus on the smaller worlds of our own influence and how best to live out the few short decades allotted to us, we realise that everyone has the power to be an agent of change – and there *is* a message of hope.

Every day people can and do change the world they live in. It's within everyone's grasp – your grasp as much as mine. We simply need to look to change ourselves. And when enough of us do so and the tipping point is reached, we will have the satisfaction of knowing we have done our bit to create a happier human race, something that will shine on way into the future. The positive ripple effect of our actions will amaze us.

Before you dismiss the idea as pie-in-the-sky optimism, take a second to reflect on the fact that humans are constantly evolving. My brain and yours are wired differently from those of people who lived in the Stone Age because each one of us is shaped by our experiences and prevailing culture. Darwin and Dawkins, working over a hundred years apart to understand what makes us tick, both identified and were a bit taken aback by altruism. If our genes are geared towards survival of the fittest and ultimately selfish, why do we instinctively rush into the traffic to save a child? Why did so many families risk prison or death by sheltering Jews – often total strangers – from the death camps during the last world war? What is it that motivates people to offer refugees a place in their homes? Our empathy is stirred when we hear victims of child trafficking speak and listen to people who have lost everything following hurricanes, floods and earthquakes. We cannot say, 'We don't know what it's like,' because we do. Our culture has already shifted.

Darwin was fascinated by how we remain kind, even at a devastating cost to ourselves. He eventually concluded that altruism, kindness *et al.* are learned behaviours, writing 'man is uniquely dominated by culture, by influences learned and handed down'. We have a unique intelligence that gives us an opportunity to thwart our selfish programming with values-driven behaviour. To quote Darwin:

> *If you wish, as I do, to build a society in which individuals cooperate generously and unselfishly towards a common good, you can expect little help from biological nature. Let us try to teach generosity and altruism because we are born selfish ... let us understand what our own selfish genes are up to because we may then at least have a chance to upset their designs.*

Richard Dawkins repeats this thought verbatim in his book *The Selfish Gene,* adding a challenge:

> *Let us try to teach generosity and altruism, because we are born selfish. Let us understand what our own selfish genes are up to, because we may then at least have the chance to upset their designs, something that no other species has ever aspired to do.*

This is a call to cultivate our generosity – what I am calling our Generous Gene! Anthropologists, psychiatrists and sociologists now agree that our lives aren't determined just by our genes but by many other factors. We have emotional as well as physical needs. Professor Walter Goldschmidt, author of *The Bridge to Humanity*, argues that we hunger for affection, bodily contact and emotion. Infants too young to know what they're doing smile, nuzzle and laugh purely to get a positive interaction with their mothers. New mothers (including mice and cats as well as humans) produce the hormone oxytocin which encourages nurturing. Toddlers too young to understand what they are doing respond with love and support when they see someone is hurt.

So, unlike Darwin's fears, our first instinct seems not to be selfish but to nurture each other and be generous! By choosing to celebrate our nurturing, generous side, we can evolve further. By practising generosity, we can challenge and change the dominant culture to one that creates a positive legacy. We can choose to celebrate our ability to connect and work for the common good. It's an inclusive process. Every single one of us can make a contribution.

By focusing on developing our Generous Gene; we will be growing that part of our psyche that has been culturally buried under the belief that a meaningful life is all about me; that success is about having lots of dosh and the ability to do anything we want to, right NOW. We can have a debate about the definition of 'success' and perhaps that's the point, because we are soft-wired for empathy and happiest when we look out for others. Our Generous Gene is something we all have within us, we just need to rediscover it.

Jeremy Rifkin is a university professor and author. I first came across his ideas in 2011 when he was promoting *The Empathic Civilization*. In less than an hour (now condensed to under 11 minutes on RSA Animates and well worth a look), he set out his vision for a positive future. Neuroscientists and behavioural experts have started challenging some of the assumptions we've taken for granted about human nature. They've discovered mirror neurons in our brains: in a nutshell, when we see someone else's pain or pleasure, we feel it too. One crying baby sets off another. Someone near us yawns and we yawn too. We empathise in the knowledge that everyone's life is fragile and often difficult.

The question Rifkin then asks is whether we are capable of extending our empathy beyond people to animals and then to our endangered planet. Think about all those animal charities and tick the first box. Reflect on the climate-change activists and tick the second box. People are showing solidarity with a cause, connecting because it awakens their sense of fairness and empathy. So the next logical step is to break down the barriers that separate us – easy with today's technology – and support each other as one interconnected family working together for the best possible solutions for every living thing: a move from independence to interdependence.

Some will dismiss this as a utopian fantasy. And OK, even the closest families fall out; and OK, given the appalling human behaviour reported at every level around the world – from embezzling politicians to merciless fighters and human traffickers – I appreciate this might seem like a long shot. But though we might in future kill each other for access to water as well as land, we might *also* make the choice to share it between us. If we accept the world and its future are scarily fragile, we can wake up and decide that we, as individuals, have the resources to tackle the challenges society faces. We have the capacity to become leaders and authors of change rather than wait for our elected politicians to delay or fudge it.

We are already seeing the impact of the power of individuals over the supposed power-holders. How will history interpret the 2015 refugee crisis and our response to it? The government of Iceland agreed to take 50 refugees and within days a Facebook campaign generated 12,000 individuals saying, 'No, we want to open our homes and we can do more.' In Germany the 'Refugees Welcome' website matched hundreds of migrants with spare rooms in shared homes, while football fans held out 'Refugees Welcome' banners at televised matches. Whilst governments hesitated – the scale of the migration was and is, after all, unprecedented – more and more individuals decided they could and should help. Before EU ministers held their emergency meeting to agree guidance for all member states, the UK government shifted its position under the weight of public opinion. Seventy-one people suffocating to death in a truck in Austria horrified us. The image of one small boy washed up on a Turkish shore lit the Generous Gene in millions of people across the world. To quote former chief rabbi Jonathan Sacks, 'It's time for human compassion to triumph.' Our natural response is to be touched by the stream of stories of persecution and images of desperation and lost hope. It is the likes of you and me who are applying pressure for a more humane and positive response.

So my call to you is to be part of this culture shift to one where we all value generosity more than profit, status symbols or financial success. We know in our hearts that it is good to be generous and kind. We experience a warm, fuzzy feeling when we've helped someone out and are touched when others are generous to us. What is love at its best but putting someone else's interests before our own? A generous life is a life well lived and a happier one. The challenge is to lead a more generous life against the peer pressure of a commercial, profit-driven world until the tipping point is reached.

Striving for growth which will destroy us is idiotic in the extreme.

We have a choice and it's time to make it.

TAKE A CANDLE

I love this story about the symbolism of the humble candle. Candles can go into symbolic overkill, so I'll keep it short.

Imagine you're in a dark room with a few others and the only light for everyone to see by is from your lit candle. Use it to light someone else's candle. Now they can see too. Your candle burns just as brightly as before, but by sharing you've more than doubled the light around you. Each lit candle lights another and the room becomes fully lit, with all the candles still burning.

Your Generous Gene – the heart-led bit of you that wants to help other people and is fundamentally good – is just waiting to be used more. What's the point of being an unlit candle? And when you start developing what feels good, even in tiny ways, I guarantee your life will grow to constantly challenge and surprise you. Teach your children and you will be wiser; be kind and you will find kindness reciprocated; spread happiness and it will come back to you. It's not difficult. Anyone can do it. Maybe the question we need to answer is: 'How on earth have we come to believe that stuff is more important than people or that "me first" is the way to live?' Developing your Generous Gene is simply giving space to what's in your heart as much as in your head.

Making the world a better place

It's action that counts. A generous life involves putting aside time to look after each other; creating quality time before Facebook time; putting real relationships before networks of thousands (how much time can you possibly spend with each one?); seeing the world through the eyes of others to overcome persecution and prejudice; reaching out in friendship to people who are lonely or finding life difficult and becoming their champion or ambassador. Pay some attention, beyond the comfortable world where water is on tap and food so plentiful we waste it, to the plight of the world's poorest and learn how simple it could be to help them.

There is hope. We are more optimistic than the news would have us believe. And we can develop our Generous Gene by sharing simple acts of kindness and compassion online, knowing that everyone gets it, and that what moves us will move others too.

Orly Wahba runs one of a growing band of online communities dedicated to changing the world by linking people through the common thread of kindness. What starts online often moves into local communities around the world. Kindness breaks down barriers, makes people feel good about themselves and others, and shines a light on the good in each of us. Orly, founder and CEO of Life Vest Inside, knows that generosity isn't about money. Giving of ourselves to others – listening, offering a hand of friendship, valuing someone else for who they are – is the greatest act of generosity. Orly says:

> *'It's something I've noticed and am now convinced about. The biggest global issue for today is people's lack of self-value and self-worth. People from any country, any age, any status; people might seem as though they have everything but they don't recognise how amazing they are. We may not be the smartest or the wealthiest, but who we are is the most amazing thing. Kindness to people helps them recognise their value, and when they value themselves, they recognise the value of others. Each person is just another piece of the puzzle. I have seen the world shift.'*

Emotional videos online have no language barriers. No one needs an interpreter to understand what's going on. Life Vest Inside's *Kindness Boomerang* film features simple, everyday acts of kindness. It went viral, has had over 21 million views and 'tons of comments'. Orly highlighted one from Libya which I find incredibly moving:

I don't think you understand how much this film has impacted me. I've watched it twenty, even a hundred times. That's the person I want to be. I cry every time. Here, they throw a gun into my hand and want me to shoot. To fight my cousin. I don't want to shoot anymore. I want to be like the people in the film. It makes me believe I can be a better person.

Great wealth, great responsibility

As individuals we each have our own sphere of influence – through parenting, school, work, amongst our neighbours, sports or social club, and how we choose to spend our money and our time. It's not the bonus, the huge annual salary or what private bankers rather quaintly call 'a liquidity event' that accompanies the sale or public offering of a company that matters; it is what people do with the proceeds. Ditto the earning capacity of hugely talented stars of screen, stage, sport and music.

Be grateful that some of us have the talent to create wealth, entertain, inspire and amuse, but know that talent doesn't exempt anyone from being part of our society. It brings with it an extra responsibility for creating change. Are those we read about using their influence to create a more balanced world? Let's have more Jamie Olivers and Joanna Lumleys, championing causes and using their celebrity to make hugely positive waves.

Everyone has a Generous Gene

Collectively, by changing what we value we can move society on. We CAN rewire our brains (literally) to create a world of you *and* me, not you *or* me. We can recapture some of the practical simplicity essential to sustain our planet. For over forty years, visionaries and global leaders have been clear on this issue. In 1973, E. F. Schumacher wrote in *Small is Beautiful* that 'infinite growth does not fit into a finite world'. Pope Francis felt the need to reiterate the thought in his 2015 Encyclical:

> *The idea of infinite or unlimited growth, which proves so attractive to economists, financiers and experts in technology ... is based on the lie that there is an infinite supply of the earth's goods, and this leads to the planet being squeezed dry at every limit.*

'Squeezed dry at every limit' is not a future anyone's going to be happy with, so we need to act now. What's your excuse? This isn't a hard thing for anyone to do. We simply need to recognise our interconnectedness and set out to create a more generous culture, wherever we are and in whatever way we can. By shifting our collective values more and more of us will find meaning and happiness because our legacy will be to regenerate the world we pass on to our children rather than exploit and damage it. Everyone can join the growing band of people participating in Random Acts of Kindness and everyone can help create a world where people are respected for being less selfish and more generous members of the human race: helping each other out because it's the right thing to do.

The seeds have already been planted. When commercial banks closed hundreds of unprofitable branches across rural Australia, Bendigo Bank was born. The communities needed a bank and decided they could share the responsibilities and rewards of a local banking system. Bendigo now has over 300 branches, provides a 32 per cent return to investors, and creates thousands of local jobs and profits that go straight back into the community: a simple win-win solution living happily alongside commercial banking giants. With the Great Barrier Reef under threat from dredging and coal mining, eleven banks refused to finance the $16.5 billion Adani mine. The reasons may have been purely commercial, but the decision is also a victory for the 2,000 people who wrote handwritten pledges to prevent it and the Wangan and Jagalingou people who challenged the mining leases granted on their land.

We need to make a real effort to learn about the issues that impact our daily lives, and then question our politicians, business people and religious leaders. Ask them the simple questions 'Why?' or 'Why not?' until we get a satisfactory answer; demand to know what they are actually actively doing to solve the problems we all know we face. Don't sit there, DO something.

By decluttering our lives we declutter our minds

Social psychologist Erich Fromm's classic *To Have or To Be?* stresses the human need to belong, and warns of the dangers of that need in a society where 'stuff' is all-powerful.

> *A society whose principles are acquisition, profit and property produces a social character orientated around having, and once the dominant pattern is established, nobody wants to be an outsider, or indeed an outcast.*

In essence, if society's cultural values put stuff first, everyone feels psychologically pressured to do the same, and we end up in a world where what we have is considered to be more important than who we are. But we can break away from that – in fact, it's essential that we do. I'm encouraged that people are making a start, but we're still far from the tipping point where 'being' is more important than 'having'; where the social character that dominates is one that values each individual's talents to contribute to a healthier, happier community.

So this is a call to start from the bottom up. That's you and me. By cultivating our Generous Gene, even in small ways, I promise you each one of us will live a happier and more fulfilled life. We can focus on regenerating the world we live in, both physically and emotionally. Living more generously is something we can learn to do and that we can instil in our children. We will be rewiring our brains to de-stress because by decluttering our lives we declutter our minds too. We will experience first-hand the benefits that come from living generous lives. We will evolve to become better than we have been, because it's never been more important and because we can. We can embrace the technology that enables us to connect worldwide and the positive power that gives us as individuals to spread the word about our Generous Gene. It is up to us.

This book will help you get started. You can start small. Where's the nearest bit of nature to you right now? Not sure?

Trick question – because it's you. You are your very own ecosystem! Be kind to yourself, eat better, develop your Generous Gene by spending more time with your friends or helping someone out and you probably won't need to visit your doctor as much.

Then work outwards from your sphere of influence. Beyond your friends, make an effort to get to know your neighbours better and help out locally. The more we allow ourselves to lean on each other for support, the more creative and generous we will be.

'Few will have the greatness to bend history itself, but each of us can work to change a small portion of events. It is from numberless diverse acts of courage and belief that human history is shaped. Each time a man stands up for an ideal,

or acts to improve the lot of others, or strikes out against injustice, he sends forth a tiny ripple of hope, and crossing each other from a million different centres of energy and daring those ripples build a current which can sweep down the mightiest walls of oppression and resistance.'

Robert F. Kennedy, US Senator

2

Living Generously

A kinder, more generous world is ours

I n 2008 the global news was about financial meltdown.
Today, global business has bounced back and grown to
unprecedented levels. Profits of the top 500 corporations
smashed new records with 27 per cent growth in 2013.
Thirteen of the top 100 global economies are corporations,
with the top five being banks. Guess how they make money?
Lending it to grow economies and businesses. Capitalism is
booming again with the gap between rich and poor widening.
For those of us who 'have', life should be good, and yet we
know power corrupts and wealth doesn't equal happiness. And
governments across the world – beyond Greece – are struggling
with debt repayments.

And we know global growth is simply not viable. Another
quote, this time from economist Kenneth Boulding, who died
more than twenty years ago now, in 1993:

*Anyone who believes in indefinite growth in anything
physical, on a physically finite planet, is either mad – or an
economist.*

Short and to the point. Another prophet we didn't listen to. It seems as though the economists are still winning, though, twenty years on: growth and a capitalist model are still the goals of those who govern and we're following like lemmings over the proverbial cliff.

I'm not pretending it's an easy call to go against the trend, especially when income, pensions and financial security are integral to the way we live every day. Paradoxically we are participating in this unsustainable system, in part because we have no idea how to get off the slippery slope. Time to work out how to align our wish to live well with a system we can live with.

New thinking

'We can't solve problems by using the same kind of thinking we used when we created them.'

Albert Einstein, physicist

'China's economy slows.' 'UK GDP rises by 0.7 per cent – back to the growth of 2008'. GDP – rising or falling – is headline news which makes and breaks governments. Riane Eisler, a social scientist whose family fled from Germany during the Second World War, is one of a growing number of people questioning why we are still using a crazy system which 'measures the wrong stuff'. The GDP measurements, she argues, skew the reality. They measure work activities that harm and take life, arms manufacturing and war, expenditure on medical bills and natural disasters. They don't measure environmental damage, suffering, hunger or poverty. So why don't we develop economic systems that give value to the real wealth of the world; the contributions made by people and nature? It's not beyond us to change the fundamentals and start measuring a caring economy with Social Wealth Indicators at the core – the life-sustaining activities of carers, volunteers, stay-at-home parents and people whose work sustains our natural world.

A light-bulb moment for me! GDP as a measurement is being challenged. The current measurement system has been around since the 1930s and needs a review. Eisler points out that countries whose policies offer high levels of benefits to families – notably Norway, Sweden and Finland – are showing enormous long-term positive returns on that investment. Hers is a call to change the GDP paradigm because caring, generous and supportive economies thrive. What are we waiting for?

We are already beginning to see the emergence of a new way of doing business. 2006 saw the start of benefit corporations – B Corps – businesses whose constitutional documents state shareholder value is not paramount, just one factor amongst others. B Corps commit to be a positive force for good in society and the environment in tandem with profit. Ice-cream giant Ben & Jerry's is an accredited B Corp. The co-founders of US crowd-funding platform Kickstarter, now valued at $1 billion, have announced they will apply for accreditation and will never go public to make millions because it's not consistent with their DNA. Unilever's CEO has gone on the record. He can see the benefits of becoming a B Corp and is looking into it, despite the complexities of accrediting a global business and the time and investment this will take. What a great vision: commercial interests working to create a world where people and the planet matter as much as profit. Companies that aim to be best *for* the world, operating transparently and in a way that makes their employees feel great. And the wonderful thing is that they are sharing what works. Great ideas get picked up.

If you haven't yet heard of SumofUs (www.sumofus.org) it's worth checking out. It's a small campaigning NGO (non-governmental organisation) that's making waves by uniting shareholders, employees and customers to challenge unethical or damaging corporate actions and government policies. Their tagline is 'Fighting for people over profits'. They're turning the heat up on pension funds to divest from fossil fuel companies and were instrumental in getting over 62,000 people to demand the investigation into alleged tax fraud by HSBC in 2014. They're now turning their attention to 'totally legal' tax avoidance schemes being facilitated by tax advisory giant KPMG. And SumofUs regularly combine forces with other campaigning groups and platforms to shout louder. Because what they uncover doesn't seem right, or good or something we can all live comfortably with once we realise what's going on. And because when we join forces we can influence the behaviour of mega corporates and hold them to account.

It's great to see some business leaders are beginning to listen. John Nelson, Chairman of Lloyd's of London, has been outspoken about the need to remedy today's lack of trust between big business and the man in the street; the legacy of the financial services debacle in 2008 and more recent 'staggering levels of corporate irresponsibility'. It's a worldwide cultural issue, he suggests. Business has to reconnect with its real purpose – servicing customers with integrity. Not riding roughshod over them. Regulation alone will not succeed; what is needed is trust, currently at an all-time low. But Nelson reckons he can see and feel more and more people questioning the capitalism that has got us to this point and looking for a new way forward for sustainable growth, with trust and integrity returning to centre stage.

If we're to develop our Generous Gene we need to make sure we motor through life feeling comfortable that we're not compromising our values by trampling over weaker members of society, even if they live on the other side of the world. We can shape a kinder, more generous world, and it's not that difficult for each of us, as individuals, to take the first step.

Let's make this personal

It's about focus. When you spend more time focusing on what you can do in your own sphere of influence, 'in giving all to the present', you'll realise you have the power to change your bit of the world, which is a very good place to start. The message is worth repeating: start small and you'll be amazed how easy it is. Practising generosity is about your state of mind more than your wallet. There are numerous acts of spontaneous generosity which are not the stuff of research or psychological studies and all that mumbo jumbo; they are just what ordinary people do when a humanitarian disaster strikes or the weather pattern swings left instead of right or you're hit by a wave of compassion and want to do something.

This is a call to do something differently, because you can; to make the world a better place, wherever you live and whatever your circumstances.

I wonder what went through Katie Cutler's mind when she read about Alan Barnes, the frail, obviously vulnerable, visually impaired, 4' 6" pensioner who'd been mugged in Gateshead in 2015? She didn't know him, but nevertheless she set up a fundraising page for someone so distressed that he couldn't face going back home. The story hit the headlines when Katie's fundraising target of £5,000 reached £330,000 – way beyond her wildest dreams. Over 21,000 people chipped in £281,000 in just four days. A totally affordable bit of cash, given in small sums from a lot of people who wanted to help and did so with just a little prompting. Katie heard of Alan's plight and did what she could. Setting up a fundraising page isn't difficult. Now she has a British Empire Medal and runs the Katie Cutler Foundation 'improving lives through acts of kindness'.

We just need to practice thinking with our hearts.

Palam Kalyanasundaram, from Tamil Nadu, South India, has

thought with his heart since he was young. Now in his seventies, he has the smiling and contented look of a man who's happy with life. A librarian for thirty-five years, he always donated his total salary to help the needy, then worked extra hours at other jobs for money to live off. He's remained a bachelor, living a simple life, and is totally unimpressed by money. 'One can get money in three possible ways. First, through earnings; secondly, through parents' earnings; and thirdly, through money donated by someone. But there's nothing more fulfilling than being able to donate money for charity out of your own earnings. Everything is a state of mind, what do we take with us when we leave planet Earth?' he said.

In 2004, he was given the US award 'Man of the Millennium', which came with a huge sum of around £3 million (30 crore rupees) attached. Naturally, he gave it all away and he now acts as a conduit between donors and people who need help. Genuine generosity is a magnet.

Quoting from Erich Fromm again, way back in 1976 he suggested we have a choice. We can either 'add ourselves up' or 'use ourselves up'. 'Adding ourselves up' is about judging ourselves by what we have, which includes the worry of losing it. That's the world in which many of us live. 'Using ourselves up' is when we create something that sets us free – because we have nothing to lose by doing, feeling, seeing, loving and being.

The one thing everyone has in common is the wish to be happy. By focusing a bit more on the positive things we can do to use ourselves up, and a bit less on adding ourselves up, we are lighting the touchpaper to live more generous lives. It's that simple.

Empathy is in our DNA

I suggest we put an end to the myth of those old-school 'survival of the fittest' rules. *Human beings are naturally generous souls, capable of outstanding and remarkable acts of generosity when we sense the need.* Empathy is built into our DNA. It's just that often we are so caught up in the hurry of living that the opportunities to help others, to give or lend an understanding ear, pass us by.

It's all too easy to find an excuse, or several excuses.

We are too busy – juggling work, family; getting through every day is a struggle; we hardly have enough time to see our friends; too many emails; too many people to keep up with. We feel overwhelmed. In part this is because we have been conditioned to think we need to be successful to be happy. Our too-busy lifestyle is one of the reasons I now spend less time listening to the news. It's depressing! I feel better with time to refocus and do more of the stuff that will develop my Generous Gene.

There's little we can do – to help the millions of people starving in Africa, or whose lives have been devastated by a tsunami, earthquake or war. I can only emphasize again: start small, and the ripple effect can make amazing things happen.

We simply become sceptical. What is the point of doing our bit to save the environment when the Chinese are building new coal-fired power stations every hour?!

We don't know how to give – or don't believe our money will really get through to the people who need it. And this list goes on: we do enough already; don't have the time; can't help everyone; it all gets stolen by corrupt governments. Finally, sorry – said with a simper – charity begins at home. We live with the constantly shifting goal of financial security into old age, for which we need to work, often harder and longer, for a career which gives us more responsibility and reward, seeing our children grow up and leave as we wonder where the time went; our lives vanishing in a maelstrom of bills needing paying and of striving for the next acquisitive goal.

I am sure there isn't a person reading this who doesn't recognise and sympathise with one or more of these barriers to living in a more generous way. But the truth is that generosity is an attitude to life. We need to challenge the cultural norms that encourage cluttered lives. Think twice before we react to sophisticated messages exhorting us to upgrade, buy 3 for 2, update the out-of-date even though it works fine, buy before the offer closes ... By focusing less on what we 'need' and more on developing compassion, an open mind and a willingness to learn and – most importantly – action, we will find we change ourselves and the ripples will help create a simpler, happier world.

What is generosity?

Generosity requires us to develop a positive and outward-looking attitude, qualities we instinctively recognise as good. We all like to be considered kind and generous and we admire generosity in others as much as we dislike people who are selfish and mean. We enjoy being generous to our family and friends when we have the opportunity and it touches the better part of us, so that something magical happens to our day. It shows and grows in our faces so we can look at a total stranger and say with confidence: 'They're a kind person.'

It's not at all intellectual. We may need practice and we might just be outside our comfort zone because it's not the social norm, but generosity is instinctive. We are moved by acts of kindness, feel compassion for the plight of others, are inspired when we witness heroic or seemingly impossible human achievements, are stirred by soppy, emotional stories and films, by happy endings and rousing music.

Generosity comes from the same spot that will spur us to do anything for one of our children or for the person with whom we fall hopelessly in love. It's the same impulse that is deeply touched when someone does something generous and thoughtful for us, or has forgiven us for a mistake we have made. It is part of the spiritual bit in us that links with compassion and love – difficult to pin down and analyse, but something we know, when used, brings joy and gives us meaning. Small acts of generosity help us stay well and keep us sane. And the sooner we get this, the better.

'Tell me and I forget, teach me and I may remember, involve me and I learn.'

Benjamin Franklin, founding father of the United States

'Franklin realised throughout his life that the only way to advance yourself is through others. How cool to realise that when you're fourteen or fifteen.'

Jessica Barratt, founder, Franklin Scholars

'One human being helping another is a very powerful thing.'

JESSICA'S STORY

When I snatch a few moments of Jessica's time over coffee, she is her usual bright and bubbly self, despite our meeting meaning she has to stop working 24/7; something she enjoys doing because she loves her work so much. 'What I do doesn't feel like work. I never get the Sunday/Monday morning blues.' Life wasn't always like this! In her own words:

'I had what I thought was my dream job managing bands and singers, but the reality of the music business was something else, so at twenty-nine I quit to volunteer for an educational NGO in Mozambique. There I discovered kids of fifteen to seventeen, still studying, who were helping younger kids out with reading and writing. This had nothing to do with the NGO. It was 100 per cent their initiative.

'I noticed very quickly the older students were more engaged, ambitious, learning empathy, improving their communication skills. They were young, relaxed and more fun than a teacher. Most of them had lots of responsibilities at home, but the skills they were learning helped them look at their future differently. One decided on a career in medicine and got a scholarship, which was a total breakthrough given her family background.

'It got me thinking. You only really understand something when you have to teach it. You don't have to be academic, it's about personal development. If I knew at their age that we all have the power to help others and that's the best way of living a better life ourselves, my life might have been totally different.

'Could this be something that could work in the UK? I knew there was lots of evidence that peer tutoring and mentoring – giving kids that responsibility – does great things for self-worth, and decided to give it a go. Hackney Pirates (a charity offering learning support) allowed me to do a pilot programme with a couple of groups of kids over a few weeks. It helped me work out how to get them engaged and keep them motivated and gave me the confidence to approach a school for a couple of one-off sessions with Year 10 and Year 7 – results also positive.

'Armed with the results of my pilots I pitched the idea to the Teach First Innovations Unit. Two of the panel were head teachers. Franklin Scholars had its first schools.

'The results amaze even me. We work with Year 7 because transition from primary to secondary school has a huge impact.

For an eleven-year-old it's a massive deal, and for kids at risk of going off the rails a precarious moment. To connect them with Year 10 students, who still remember what it was like three years ago, but are old enough to be real and responsible role models, is genuinely helpful.

'We have a totally inclusive recruitment process for our coaches ('coaches' works better than 'mentors' – everyone knows a great athlete has a great coach) and make sure less confident students know they can apply. The kids genuinely want to help out. Not one of last year's 120 recruits dropped out, even though they commit to an hour a week for a full year over their normal schoolwork. They show amazing resilience and perseverance. Even when the younger kids don't engage immediately, they stick with it and end up with really strong relationships.

'The training is about self-awareness, empathy, communication. They learn patience, humility, to see things from others' perspectives; they develop an inner self-confidence. The feedback is that this spills over to life outside. They start to "think Franklin Scholars in my head"; "Now if I see someone fall over in the street I'll help". And helping others with their issues helps them sort out their own.

'We use the same inclusive approach with Year 7s. Having a coach mustn't badge you as a failure. The intro session is fun and games, ending with a "speed networking" session where we give a topic for everyone to discuss. Both groups of kids answer questions which help identify who they think they would like to pair up with.

'We have doubled the number of pupils and schools involved in our second year and plan to double again next year. Grades for both ages are improving. Teachers are noticing leadership skills developing and kids becoming more resilient. Every single Year 10 student involved has said they'll be more likely to help others in the future. Franklin Scholars is growing by word of mouth. The first Franklin Scholars, now in Year 11, are helping recruit and train the next cohort.'

Jessica's trying to create 'a bit of a movement'. Being a Franklin Scholar is part of a bigger thing. In Jessica's own words: 'It's great for Scholars in north-west England to know they are part of a group in another part of the country and will share in a massive graduation event. Teenage years are about impressing others, belonging, being cool. When they realise they can help another, some of the stuff they worry about isn't that important. Once a Franklin Scholar, always a Franklin Scholar. One human being helping another is a very powerful thing. As for myself, I'm a million times happier.'

What Jessica knows is that being a Franklin Scholar changes people. When we put ourselves first, whether as individuals or nations, and succumb to our selfish gene, we create inequality and suffering. When we work together towards a common goal we can achieve truly great things. As more of us pack this planet the latest buzzwords are 'collaboration' and 'community'. Peacemaking starts with communication to build understanding. It cannot come a moment too soon, for even as we commemorate and mourn the impact of wars, new leaders and generations continue to fight for control or to annihilate their enemies, and in the confusion of conflict more innocent women and children die than those who carry arms. Pooling our talents to solve problems together is an infinitely more constructive way to build a better world.

Generous by nature

I believe that we are all generous by nature. We've just been temporarily brainwashed. Generosity is a natural human instinct as well as a positive approach to living. It is taking an active interest in the world outside our immediate existence. It is something we can also cultivate. Our brains are only 25 per cent of their final size when we are born. In the first three years of life, a baby's exposure to the world shapes literally billions of connections in his or her brain. And it doesn't stop there. Throughout our lives, our neural connections shift and change. Something neuroscientists call plasticity. The environment we live in has an enormous influence on our brains and how we see life.

Richard Davidson is a highly respected professor of psychology and psychiatry. He's spent years in the lab attaching electrodes to people's skulls to measure their brain activity and he knows, because he and his team have scientifically validated data, that generosity (doing something for others) activates circuits in our brains that create more lasting positive change than anything else studied. The circuits that create a sense of well-being.

It's a simplification to say we become what we focus on, but let's keep to that level.

Long before 'civilisation' arrived, the earliest hunter-gatherer societies (which existed for 85,000 years before agriculture started some 12,000 years ago) were successful because they developed through co-operation and collective decision-making. Hunting, foraging, cooking, childcare and building were allocated to match people's skills, experience and aptitude. There was no personal acquisition, no social or power-based hierarchy. Men and women contributed in different ways at different life stages and were equally valued. Different people would take the lead depending on what needed to be done. In short, without the current mindset of 'having', they created a generous, successful, sharing community.

By contrast, most of the societies we recognise today as 'developed' and 'civilised' are typified by the constant and relentless pressure to become independent and financially secure (whatever that means), and by the growth of consumerism – to the point where we are encouraged to shop till we drop and to judge people by visible signs of success rather than by who they are, even though we know that the trappings of success are hollow compared to the joy of a loving family life.

In becoming consumers, we have lost the generosity that is natural to us – what we might recognise as the generosity of the poor; the generosity of our hunter-gatherer ancestors. We have created societies with growing inequality of wealth. When Oxfam publicises the statistic that the world's 85 richest people own the same wealth as the 3.5 billion poorest, something unhealthy is going on. When the corporate profit motive rides roughshod over people's well-being, we need to demand change. The great thing is: we can do it ourselves, just by starting small.

By focusing on our self-worth, not our net worth, we can change ourselves, our lives and potentially the way the neurons in our brains connect. If you have enough stuff, it won't do you any harm at all to regularly give away a little of your income or wealth to help people less fortunate than yourself, and benefit from a nice warm feeling of positive satisfaction in so doing. If you focus less on acquiring things, you worry less about losing (or insuring, breaking, upgrading) them, and have more space in your life to value friendships, sharing, love and the joy of interdependence. If you want to make the streets you live in friendlier and more caring, start collaborating and experimenting and you will find that you can.

'I believe we have a fundamental human need to give. We all need help in our own lives, we all need to give. At a funeral or memorial service, you never hear people say, "He made a lot of money, he had three boats." You hear, "He was generous, sincere, always had time for people." Those are the things

43

that we value in others and we value them in ourselves. We feel better for giving.'

David Robinson, founder, Community Links and
We Are What We Do

How to be generous: an open heart, an open hand and an open mind

If the word 'generosity' is too linked in your mind with cash, focus on being kind. Opening our hearts gives us an opportunity to pause, a chance to think about others, to love them and to look for ways to care for them, without making judgements or expecting to receive anything in return.

A KNOWN FACE, A KIND WORD: TERRY'S STORY

Terry is a gardener; for many years he played for his village football team and he is now a member of the local pub bowling league. He still lives in the Somerset village where he grew up, which – by some wonderful stroke of fate – is also the village to which my parents finally moved.

He is a very normal bloke ... except for his exceptional generosity, which he dismisses with an embarrassed smile. One of his jobs was to help my elderly parents with their garden, mowing the lawn and keeping the hedges down when it became too much for them. For the last ten years of my mother's life, when she was in her eighties and nineties and living alone, he was also her rock.

Officially, Terry came once a week for a couple of hours. Unofficially, he popped in twice a day. Every day. Just passing by for a cup of tea at around five and back again at around eight

44

for 'the final round-up'. Doors locked, cats fed, curtains closed, mother safe and OK. In winter, the hot-water bottle would be filled and the bed warmed (for 'health and safety' reasons, this was outside the remit of the visiting carers). At one stage, the hard-pressed local authority suggested they cut back on the evening carers' visits because 'your gardener comes, doesn't he?' 'Yes, but it's not his job or his responsibility. He does it out of the kindness of his heart,' my mother would respond. And we didn't pay him, because time and again he refused the offer.

When my mother's daily routine reduced to moving between her bedroom and the armchair, Terry was the constant presence in her life. Much more constant than I was able to be, living a hundred-plus miles away. A known face, a kind word. Every day, twice a day, as regular as clockwork.

My phone would ring: 'Terry's late, do you think he's alright?' or: 'I'm worried about Terry, he hasn't come yet.' I can count on the fingers of one hand the days he didn't come round without letting my mother know in advance – and there was always a reason, such as there had been a wedding or a funeral which had lasted longer than expected.

Thank you, Terry. I am forever indebted to you, though you will brush away the compliment. You are a truly generous gentleman in every way.

Encouraging people is generosity. Practise giving compliments: telling people they are fab, talented, kind and that they can win if they keep going. So often words of encouragement given at a critical moment provide the spark we need to carry on with our hopes and plans and dreams, to move forward and not give up. Telling someone you believe in them is incredibly powerful and generous.

An open hand invites us to get off our backsides and do something, to be proactive in helping others, to come alongside when they need us and let go when they don't.

Sharing what you have with others is generosity, and it's brilliant to see the term 'sharing economy' now in general use. First and foremost, share your time and connect. Someone who is housebound or ill will be counting the time in slow motion until the next person makes them aware they're not forgotten, even if it's only by email. Practise sharing a meal (there's probably no need to buy extra – it'll go round), your expertise, your hospitality or even a bed for the night. No cost at all. Share skills and experience; expand the babysitting circle to include the car-share club and the DIY tool-share.

An open mind teaches us to listen, to learn and to look at people and their problems from a different and more compassionate angle. To refrain from making judgemental or daft remarks, but to hear and acknowledge others' points of view – and that includes your children's. This is possibly the most important quality needed to lead a generous life.

Rewarding yourself is generosity. It's hugely important to be kind to yourself, buy yourself a treat as pure self-indulgence or as a reward for something you know you've achieved; especially if no one else has noticed. It warms up your Generous Gene! Of more practical use is to learn how to forgive yourself for falling short; refusing to beat yourself up for your own perceived weaknesses; for not getting the job you really wanted; for your share of the breakdown of a relationship. Practise empathy with yourself! Accept yourself for what you are and where you're at. Give yourself a break and move on. We all fail sometimes, but to dwell on a mistake is to remain anchored in the past.

'We're all different. You can do things that I can't do. I can do things that you can't do. And that's just fine.

'*In our African culture, there is something very difficult to put into English – Ubuntu. Ubuntu speaks about the essence of being human. We say that a person is a person through other persons ... that it is impossible to be human as a solitary individual ... that we are created for interdependence, and my humanity is caught up in your humanity. I need you to be all you can be in order for me to become all I can be. Forgiveness is therefore not altruistic, but is instead the best form of self-interest. Conversely, a person who dehumanises another is also dehumanised.*'

Archbishop Desmond Tutu, chair of South Africa's Truth
and Reconciliation Commission

Forgiveness is generosity. Forgiveness and moving on should be no-brainers, but are perhaps the toughest of all generous acts. Forgiving people for things they have said or done (or things you think they have said or done) that have made you angry, or perhaps hurt you, is hugely difficult and takes great courage. Yet it can also be extremely hard to forgive yourself.

There is a simple truth about forgiveness – it is an act of choice. You can choose to forgive someone for something they have done, and in so doing feel the weight lift off your shoulders, enabling you to move on. Or you can refuse forgiveness and carry the mistrust or hatred with you to your grave. Ultimately, there is nothing that is unforgiveable, as Mpho's story reveals.

LIFE WITHOUT FEAR OR HATRED: MPHO'S STORY

I was privileged to hear Mpho Tutu talk about forgiveness after the publication of *The Book of Forgiving*, which she co-authored with her father, Desmond Tutu. Interviewed by

Jeremy Paxman, she was asked, 'Are there any circumstances you could not forgive?' Paxman knew as he asked the question that a woman named Angela, someone Mpho loved, had been murdered whilst living with her family.

Her answer came back unequivocally along the following lines: 'Forgiveness is ultimately a selfish act. It may be incredibly difficult, but I forgive for healing for myself, so that I can live my life without fear and hatred defining it.'

After he endured twenty-seven years in jail, most people expected Nelson Mandela to emerge hungry for revenge. But instead of retribution, he urged his own people to work for reconciliation. And, leading by example, he invited his former jailer to attend his presidential inauguration as a VIP guest.

Learning to forgive is one of the hardest things to do, but also one of the most generous and liberating.

Develop your Generous Gene

Live Ubuntu. Find your place in the world through what you do for others and encourage everyone younger than you to do the same.

Start small and watch for the ripple effect. Keep tabs on the feedback you get when you do something kind – however small – or go out of your way to listen or to help. Then pause and think about how that makes you feel and give yourself a pat on the back for developing your Generous Gene. **Rewarding yourself** is important.

Be proactive. Reach out to help when you see help is needed, back off when it's not, listen without judging.

Be open. Share your story, trust people, be as authentic and true to yourself as it is possible to be. And encourage others to be true to themselves too.

Learn to forgive. Wipe the slate clean, even when it's difficult, remembering that forgiveness is your choice to move forward and leave bitterness behind.

3

Generosity and Ethics

'Always do right. This will gratify some people
and astonish the rest.'

Mark Twain, author

If we become what we focus on, it follows there has to be a
radical shift in some of the systems we accept as part of everyday
life today because 'it's just the way it is'. Maybe our conscience
pricks us but we don't know how we can begin to work for change.
But to create a more generous world we need to be vocal about
it. Now, more than ever before, collective public opinion makes
it possible for individuals to challenge the unethical behaviour of
mighty institutions and people in positions of power.

Generous work

I wonder if we'll always accept that people seem to be paid
in inverse proportion to their value to society? How can this
be right? It's hardly surprising that ordinary men and women
get very angry when bankers and business leaders receive huge
bonuses for betting on the derivatives market, or advising on the
hostile takeovers of companies, or resigning when their leadership has failed yet still bag compensation packages worth several
million. Does financial wizardry and market manipulation really

reflect what we value most in life? As Warren Buffett points out, how can it be fair for him (annual income *c.* $46m/£28m) to pay tax at 17.7 per cent when his secretary, on an above-average income of $60,000 (roughly £39,000) is taxed at 30 per cent?

I can't be the only one who sighs inwardly when another senior executive or politician is exposed by the media and offers the lame excuse of 'What I did was within the rules'. Was it within the spirit of the rules? Or was there a tiny little loophole they managed to squeeze through? Deep down in their gut are they comfortable their actions were right? Or was the motivation more about personal gain, meeting a delivery target or corporate profit? Or the thrill of outsmarting the system? Wouldn't it be wonderful to reach a tipping point where the censure of public opinion and the threat of transparency made people think long and hard before trying to get away with it because, as we all know, prevention is better than cure?

As we weigh up the pros and cons of the work we do to get through life and the decisions we make along the way, it's worth remembering that numerous studies have found that once you're paid fairly, other motivators kick in. What will your life's work be worth to you and to others when you look back on it? Reward the wealth creators and innovators, but also show our support for a more caring world by valuing those who work in jobs that make everyday life better for the rest of us. How do you assess the contribution of a fireman against that of an insurance underwriter in your life? You are likely to find yourself relying on rescue services after a car crash, or fire services should your chip pan catch fire and with it your house. When a new baby is due, nurses, doctors and midwives are there for you, helping bring 'the most beautiful baby ever born' into the world.

Our children are taught, sometimes against all the odds, by teachers hoping to inspire each child to learn, read, write and discover their talents so they become confident adults. Social workers – who so often get a bad press – work unbelievably long hours to support incredibly vulnerable people, the very people we too often turn away from as 'not our problem'. NHS Careers describes the job as 'forming relationships with people and assisting them to live more successfully within their communities by helping them find solutions to their problems'. As we turn away, our taxes pay professionals to sort out issues on our doorstep.

The list goes on: police officers, prison officers, hospital cleaners and porters, rubbish collectors, road sweepers – we need to value them all. We'd notice soon enough if our rubbish wasn't collected. We don't hesitate to complain if the hospital toilet isn't pristine. The average salary for a refuse collector is £15,000–£18,000 a year for a 40-hour week. The specialist paramedic who could save your life in an ambulance has a starting salary of £21,478 (rising to almost £29,000 at the top of the pay scale). When set against our national average wage of £24,648, the implication is that it must be an average job – something I think we would all agree could not be further from the truth.

If you are lucky and talented enough to have a highly paid job, accept it comes with an extra responsibility to act ethically, with integrity. By doing what is right you will be generous to those who've helped you along the way, nursed you when you were sick, inspired you when you were young, encouraged you when you were down but who are quite likely living modest lives on much lower salaries. If you notice unethical behaviour, challenge the management, change your job, start a public petition, shop elsewhere. Be the person you want to be. Gradually, bit by bit, things will change.

Intellectual generosity: might isn't always right

There seems to be some kind of unwritten law that deliberately daft and controversial views and offensive opinions generate more media coverage than generous views and intelligent debate. Our legal and political systems are adversarial. It is the art of journalism to expose different views to get a debate going, and to demand 'Yes' and 'No' answers even when most of us know the goalposts are rapidly changing. How dull it is when people agree.

There are highly qualified experts in every corner of life whom we feel unqualified to challenge. Lawyers with bundles of papers stacking up to dispose of less well-researched arguments. Did we really need to wait until there was an equally thick pile of evidence before we realised apartheid could never be morally justified? Are the indigenous peoples coming together to fight the oil and gas industries and protect their lands to be sidelined because of smaller legal teams? These are just normal people with a cause to fight, who can go on to achieve remarkable victories despite their faults and in face of bitter opposition from those paid to oppose; including vested interests and lobbyists. William Wilberforce, Martin Luther King, Gandhi, Nelson Mandela and many others are now heroes where once they struggled to effect change, suffered greatly for their views and were attacked continuously by those defending the status quo. What will history make of WikiLeaks or Edward Snowden?

Controversy outsells a good-news story every time. When Mother Teresa died, a small section of the media had a field day. What she had achieved, and the love she was given by people across the world, was tarnished by stories of her accepting money from undesirable sources and being photographed holding hands with Michèle Duvalier, wife of former Haitian dictator Jean-Claude Duvalier. She took a strong stand against birth control and abortion. She didn't believe women should be priests. Controversial views to hold in the 1990s.

Thankfully, the majority of people chose to remember the good she had done and ignore the rest. Mother Teresa had done too much, made too much of a difference for journalists to change our view. No one is perfect. Her life consisted of large amounts of determination, hard work and commitment and she stuck to her beliefs. Final answer.

Faith and secular ethics

'The wise man does not lay up his own treasures. The more he gives to others, the more he has for his own.'

Lao Tzu, Chinese philosopher

I was one of the 2,000 people packed into a theatre to hear the Dalai Lama speak when he visited London in 2015. As a life-long practising Buddhist his message is one of connection, of how we are all the same under our skin. He embraces other speakers on the stage with warm, slow hugs and talks of the global responsibility all seven billion of us have for each other. A man of faith, he believes that people of all faiths and none should show love to each other, because love and friendship generate trust and trust generates the honesty to have the conversations about what really matters in life. If faith divides us, love will unite us. This is why he has created the term 'secular ethics' as a way of connecting the neuroscientists, philosophers, people of all faiths and none on an equal footing; an inclusive approach to promote the compassion and generosity which scientific evidence has now confirmed is great for our health.

Compassion and generosity have been woven into human history and promoted by all religions and great thinkers since time began. It's not news that life is better when we live generously, we just have to do it. Every faith promotes generosity and 85 per cent of us say faith is part of our lives. So time to get a grip!

Do unto others as you would have them do unto you.

Gospel of Matthew, 7:12

This has become known as The Golden Rule. Very few people, whatever their faith or lack of it, disagree. Generosity is a virtue people are happy to endorse, whether we have a faith or are confirmed atheists or whether – and this group numbers millions throughout the world – we simply 'don't know'. Generosity is admired and practised in all cultures and all faiths and is non-denominational.

Anthropologists and scientists have long argued that knowledge would bring about an end to faith. Faith only existed because we couldn't explain, or didn't know, what science was bound to explain; it was based on ignorance and superstition. Yet mystery continues to be found everywhere, even as we continue to evolve and even as scientists develop the capacity to genetically modify our foods and our embryos and explore our brains in ways that were impossible to imagine just a few decades ago. Those who predicted the death of faith have been proved wrong. Given global events, it's necessary to separate out faith from religions, because what we experience as religious fundamentalism isn't justified by faith in a god or higher being. It seems illogical that in the twenty-first century Christianity is keeping pace with the growth in global population and Islam is growing faster. There are now over 7.2 billion people in the world (keep adding 120,000 more births than deaths every day), of which about 2.1 billion people are Christians, 1.6 billion Muslims, 1 billion Hindus and 400 million Buddhists, plus millions more who ascribe to numerous smaller faith groups. According to Wikipedia, the secular non-believers/atheists number 1.1 billion.

Assuming the stats give a reasonably accurate picture, around 85 per cent of people claim to have faith and around 70 per cent belong to one of the major world faiths. It seems we need faith as much as we ever did to make sense of our world.

Everyone acknowledges they are more than a bundle of flesh and bones – there is something in each of us that speaks to a spiritual element we don't quite understand. A significant majority believe in a higher being or beings who created the universe and who answer prayers. We cannot explain love by science even when we can measure the changes it creates in us. We know that positivity speeds recovery from mental illness and cancers, but not exactly how. The major world faiths are keeping pace with global population growth, not fading away. They have shaped history and have endured, and there is no evidence at all to show their influence is now diminishing, despite today's scientific accomplishments and vocal challengers.

Perhaps we need reminding that all world faiths have at their heart similar teachings about helping less fortunate members of society. All place great emphasis on generosity, giving both money and love, quietly and with humility.

In Judaism, *Tzedakah* (literally 'righteousness') is more than charity. The word's root is related to justice and the obligation of *Tzedakah* rests on everyone, rich and poor alike. Moses Maimonides, the greatest Jewish thinker of the entire pre-modern period – philosopher, physician, legal and ethics scholar – devised eight levels of *Tzedakah*. The highest level enables a person to become self-sufficient by providing him/her with a job or other means of financial support. The next four champion generosity and anonymity, excluding the possibility of being rewarded by being known as generous. Thereafter, real generosity slips – the donor gives graciously and sufficiently but only after being asked; the donor gives cheerfully, but less than is appropriate; the giver gives begrudgingly and less than is needed.

Maimonides's thinking on generosity can be summed up briefly. A person who gives only after being asked is not really generous; giving less than is appropriate is mean; giving begrudgingly makes you not a nice person. He taught that the method of giving charity is an integral part of charity itself.

One of the most important principles of Islam is that everything belongs to Allah and that wealth is held by human beings in trust. One of the five pillars of Islam, *Zakat*, meaning both 'purification' and 'growth', is firmly established in the Qur'an as obligatory. It is the amount of money that every mentally stable, free and financially able Muslim, male or female, has to pay to support specific categories of people. Setting aside a proportion of what you have purifies you. Cutting back on your needs balances and encourages new growth. For most Muslims, this involves an annual payment of 2.5 per cent of capital.

Generosity's cultural base is also strong. One of the characteristics of Arab society generosity is found in its strongest form in Bedouin culture. Bedouin are most famous for their hospitality or *diyafa*. One of their core values, rooted in the harshness of desert life, is never to turn a traveller away. Any stranger, even an enemy, can approach a tent and be sure of three days' board, lodging and protection, after which he may leave in peace. Bedouin will always offer their guest a rich meal, even if they have to slaughter their last sheep or borrow from neighbours to do it. Their honour is bound by their hospitality and lavish generosity.

Hindu culture teaches that God could come to visit your home, and when He does He will come as a stranger to whom you must offer food and shelter. If you really want to know God, He is in the strangers – so no one should leave your home without at least a glass of water.

'Teach this triple truth to all: a generous heart, kind speech and a life of service and compassion are the things which renew humanity.'

Buddha

The Buddhist concept of sympathetic joy arises when someone regards all human beings with loving kindness and rejoices in their good fortune. By overcoming resentment, envy and jealousy, and finding inspiration in the happiness and accomplishment of others, an individual can begin to understand how solid and genuine shared happiness is. Buddha saw *dana* – generosity of spirit, giving and receiving from the heart – as both the generous act of giving and the gift itself. In Buddhism, generosity and kindness are skills and practices to be cultivated and nurtured for us all to thrive.

Jesus, too, was a believer in generosity. Take the story of the widow's mite, as told in Luke's gospel (Ch.21, v.1–4):

Jesus sat down opposite the place where the offerings were put and watched the crowd putting their money into the temple treasure. Many rich people threw in large amounts. But a poor widow came and put in two very small copper coins, worth only a fraction of a penny.

Calling his disciples to him, Jesus said, 'I tell you the truth, this poor widow has put more into the treasury than all the others. They gave out of their wealth; but she, out of her poverty, put in everything – all she had to live on.'

This is a call to reckless generosity: generosity without limits. St Paul, largely responsible for creating the early Christian church, spread the word too: 'Whoever sows sparingly will also reap sparingly, and whoever sows generously will reap generously.'

Develop your Generous Gene

Make sure work and your values line up. You're the decision maker here. If you disagree with the ethics where you work, challenge them or move on. If you are in charge, set the values and work for everyone to live up to them. A close friend owns a small horticulture business. When the weather's dire there's no profit. Even in a good year it's a highly competitive environment for a small operator, but the business survives because my friend really cares for his workforce and they pull out all the stops for him too. People before profit is a key value of that business.

Don't accept might is right. There's a wonderful YouTube video featuring the song 'United Breaks Guitars'. Dave Carroll's guitar was broken when he flew with United Airlines. Unable to get them to pay any compensation he wrote the song, put it on YouTube and almost immediately won a victory over his Goliath. Bet United won't do that again. Dave's video has now had over 15 million views.

Check out product sourcing. Removing our custom from unethically sourced products and unethically run businesses is the surest way to change them. To make this manageable just think of something you buy regularly and research it. Major campaigning organisations will have got there before you, so add your voice and spend your money somewhere else.

Help out. Many hard-pressed services will be freed up a little when we look out for each other – especially those who are lonely or struggling with mental health.

Remember to treat others with love. Whether you're a person of faith or have no faith at all.

4

The Secrets of Happiness

'Happiness is not something ready-made.
It comes from your own actions.'

Dalai Lama XIV

Ask anyone what they want most from life and the answer is simple and consistent. What we want for ourselves and the people we love is to be happy and fulfilled. And happiness is not really about wealth. Money helps, but not nearly as much as most of us think. The designer wardrobe, yacht, exotic holidays and financial freedom to do whatever we want whenever we want are way down the pecking order. The economic argument that more money will make you happier has been dumped by most statisticians some time ago.

When you have a relatively modest amount to live off, the secret to happiness is no secret. We thrive through finding purpose in our lives and meaningful relationships – and not just with those closest to us, but with colleagues at work, neighbours and acquaintances. People need people. A greeting as you pass someone in the street, a few words as you pay for your groceries, are part of the warp and weft of a happy life. Doing your bit to express *Ubuntu*: you are a better person through your interactions with other people. Live life with generosity to the fore and I promise you'll be a happier bunny!

It's quite clear we're interested in finding the magic bullet. When I last looked, Amazon had over 45,000 books with 'happiness' in the title. There's more and more scientific research and monitoring being done on this subject. Academics are now looking into inter-generational well-being. What does this generation need to do to ensure the next generation is OK? The assumption is that we don't want our legacy to reduce their well-being. So policies that ignore climate change, allow people to wreak havoc with our natural resources, wreck our health or shorten future generations' life expectancy should be no go.

We have a 'current happiness' problem. The UK and USA have been getting richer, but not happier, for the last sixty years. So we need to question why we carry on along a trajectory that doesn't work and is creating massive issues for the future of the planet. Surely we can change the direction of the herd?

Being kind, I'd say that message is making progress – but it's still a long way from the top of the political agenda. In 2012 the UN held its first-ever conference on happiness and in 2013 the World Happiness Report was published with data from 149 countries. The OECD, which was established to gather economic data across 34 countries, is now looking at happiness measures as well. This shouldn't surprise us, as the UN forecasts that simply continuing the current global population and consumption trends (growth) will need the equivalent of two Earths to support humanity by the 2030s. Economists are also now turning their attention to how we might improve policies beyond measuring GDP, so we don't all need to evacuate to Mars. Let's generate a conversation about Social Wealth Indicators as a better measure than GDP to help them on their way.

What makes societies happy?

Happiness is also being taken seriously because whilst we're getting richer, we're experiencing increasing levels of depression and anxiety. With around one in five of us suffering from a mental health issue at some stage of our lives, being better off doesn't make anyone immune. Mental health is a bigger issue than physical health, and of course the two can't be separated. The World Health Organization suggests a figure of 450 million sufferers worldwide, with nearly a million people taking their own lives every year. We live in an unhappy world.

Lord Richard Layard, one of the authors of the UN Happiness Report, is an economist. He challenges us to answer the question: 'What kind of society do we want to live in?' His answer is that we should aim to create societies with the greatest happiness and least misery; he argues that there's an inextricable link between our personal happiness and a happy society and that to be truly happy we need to care deeply for the happiness of others. James Maskell, a clinical instructor at George Washington University, has, over years of research, concluded that the secret to a long and healthy life is more about being part of a strong community than medicine. If you want to stay happy and well, your best plan could be to move – or to focus on making your neighbourhood more neighbourly. Not such a bad plan to reduce the spiralling costs of medical intervention around the world. Yet a government whose job was to reduce suffering and create an environment that would promote health and happiness would need to be radically different to those we see at work today.

KINDNESS KEEPS THE WORLD AFLOAT: ORLY'S STORY

Orly Wahba's message is that kindness and compassion have a power and magic that can change the world. For a start, they cost nothing; they're accessible to every single one of us; they're infectious; and, finally, the impact of a single act ripples outwards.

Orly herself exudes energy and confidence. A native New York, she reckons that part of her DNA has always been to connect people together, but it was as a middle-school teacher that she started to address her pupils' low self-esteem. She wanted to open their eyes so they'd recognise how valued they were. 'Kindness is something that's difficult to express, so for the kids in school I put together some very simple Acts of Kindness cards: a deck with lots of different small actions they could do easily. Shaking someone's hand is a kindness; opening the door for someone.' It was a simple solution that worked. The kids were energised. They started to see the ripple effect. They felt better about themselves. And happier.

And as Orly experienced the feelings she had through her own altruism – as she put it, 'Small acts that left an imprint on my heart' – she knew she wanted to share something with the world that was incredibly hard to articulate. Her answer was *Kindness Boomerang*, a film she hoped 'a few people would stumble on' when she posted it on YouTube. Over 21 million have stumbled on it so far and it's changing lives in very powerful ways.

'I've seen the world shift,' Orly says. 'When people "like" the YouTube video we follow up – and when they leave comments too. I love talking to people. Making people feel good is my favourite thing in the world. The film's impact has been way over anything I could have hoped for. I know it's saved people who were suicidal.'

Now, through heading up the charity she created (Life Vest Inside, tagline: 'Kindness keeps the world afloat'), Orly's doing more than her bit to unite the world through kindness. There are already Kindness Ambassadors in 80 cities around the world, education programmes and global street-dance events. Her mantra is to move from inspiration to action. Most people connected with Life Vest Inside are volunteers.

But what about persecution, suffering, religious wars? What about the atrocities we know are happening and the people perpetrating them? Isn't a world full of kindness an impossible dream?

'Religion is a source of animosity and people aren't always good. We've tried war. Maybe we should try something else,' is Orly's answer. 'A key we've not seen. Research all the religions and the common key is kindness. God wanting us to kill in his name doesn't sound right.

'It's the interpretation that's the issue. I see our job as taking down walls, making everyone feel comfortable and accepted. We operate an open platform for everyone. Part of the work I do is to mediate conflict by getting people of different faiths to see each other's perspectives; to recognise difference isn't a reason for war. People don't want war and aggression in their lives and if we can just nudge them to move forward we'll see a big change. Each person is another piece in the puzzle. At the end of the conversation, I often hear: "Please don't stop what you're doing. It helps me believe a better world is possible."'

Happiness is up to us, not our politicians

A better, kinder and happier world. We have it in us to evolve to a different level by developing our Generous Gene. And the great thing about happiness is that it's up to us, not anyone else. We have the ability to improve our own levels of happiness. As Orly says, as the Dalai Lama has already said: *we just need to act.*

Paul Zak, an economist and scientist, has become known primarily for his research into the oxytocin hormone (mentioned in Chapter 1 in relation to nurturing), which our brain releases when we empathise with others. Zak's 'prescription' to release the oxytocin (which helps to create the empathy needed for positive relationships, which in turn will make us happier) is eight hugs a day! I like hugs so I, for one, am up for that.

What makes children happy?

While scientists don't know exactly how it works, all agree oxytocin is a hormone that influences mood, and how we feel about life is what makes us happy. And as we can learn the disciplines that train our minds to be happy, there's no excuse for not starting early in life. The important bit for all parents to know is that looking after your child's emotional health is the best way to increase the odds of nurturing his or her happiness in adult life. Of course education is important, but if you're intent on cramming as much learning as you can into your children as early as possible, or worrying about your sports-crazy/lazy/non-academic offspring, relax, as there's good news. Academic achievement is the lowest predictor of adult happiness. The London School of Economics has been following thousands of people over decades; this is thorough research writ large. Rather than good grades, character and resilience are what's needed. And resilience *can* also be taught – indeed, *is* being taught in schools today. Just one workshop a week helps relieve depression, and improves attendance *and* academic achievement. And the kids say they enjoy the sessions. They learn how to cope in adversity, how to challenge negativity, how to problem-solve in social settings, how to relax. And guess what? They're more positive about themselves and life and their grades go up! If your local nursery school hasn't cottoned on to the 'Kindness Curriculum' yet, have a word with them. And just a few minutes of meditation a day makes kids calmer, happier and more caring.

'Our education system should help children to develop the character traits that underpin a happy and meaningful life – including empathy, generosity, resilience and compassion. Because the values that our children learn today don't just shape their future lives, they determine the destiny of our society.'

Sir Anthony Seldon, headmaster, Wellington College 2006–2013

When a whole set of kids learn skills together, no one gets left out in the playground and bullying stops. Talking of bullying, why not follow the lead of John Stainer Primary School, where Anti-Bullying Week has morphed into It's Cool to be Kind Week?

Rather than nagging your child about school reports, exams and a decent degree (or on the even more basic level I am guilty of, nagging about tidying up), enjoy the change you'll notice when you teach them simple meditation. At the end of the day, being there for your kid's emotional upheavals, scrapes and crises and helping them to cope is at least as important – I'd suggest more important – as sending them off for an extra tutorial.

IT'S COOL TO BE KIND: ADRIAN'S STORY

What happens when you're the PSHE (personal, social, health and economic education) co-ordinator at a primary school and have to take the lead on Anti-Bullying Week? Adrian Bethune found himself on the spot and he wasn't keen on the title of the campaign. The word 'bullying' has a negative ring to it, after all, so Adrian got the OK to rename it: 'It's Cool to be Kind Week'.

'Everyone from Reception to Year 6 had the same home-work,' he explains. 'We turned it into a whole school project. They had to carry out a random act of kindness and capture it somehow – a drawing, a photo, writing it down – and then reflect on how they felt about it and how the recipient felt. Everyone completed it (not always the case with homework!) with some really touching examples: "I gave my baby brother a bath to give Mum a rest" and "I got the paper for my neighbour who's elderly and disabled". The staff's job during the week was to notice when the kids were being kind and acknowledge it. "Thanks for opening the door," that sort of thing. We got the dreaded Ofsted call on the Tuesday. The inspectors arrived on Wednesday and the kids were just incredible, offering to carry their bags, opening doors ... we got an "Outstanding"!

'The second year, we did the same thing and it lost a bit of the magic, so Year 3 brainstormed ideas. Each class had to do something for the community. "Community" for the younger kids was the wider school – they told jokes to other year groups and gave shoulder massages to the teachers. The older kids started doing stuff outside school – handing out the *Metro* to commuters with kind notes on them made a big impact – and we started getting emails with really great feedback. Such a little thing lifted people's days. So I roped in a couple of teachers and between us we agreed to do covert Random Acts of Kindness for every member of staff. It was great because they always thought it was me and I could honestly deny it. And we put up a Good Deed Feed in reception – loads of Post-it Notes which kids, parents and visitors stopped to read. It stayed up till the end of term.

'I genuinely believe the children think more about other people than just themselves instinctively now. Children growing up find it hard to have a perspective about how they fit into the world. Often, it's all about them because that's all they know. "It's Cool to be Kind Week" has widened their perspective, given them a purpose which is really positive. And there's no bullying.'

How to be happy at work

Nearly all of us need to earn a living, ideally by doing something we enjoy. So what do businesses need to do for their employees to flourish?

There is now plenty of evidence challenging the presumption that you need to pay highly competitive salaries to attract the best talent. Yes, people need to be paid enough to feel they are being treated fairly, and fairness is about being rewarded at a similar level to others doing roughly the same job. When a job's routine and simple, fair pay is important, but the more complicated the job, the less individual financial incentives work.

Dan Pink is an author and researcher who suggests that the whole idea that people respond to incentives and bonuses is flawed, because it's based on the assumption that we are passive by nature, motivated by obvious external rewards, rather than active, more powerfully motivated by doing something because we feel it's important and matters. His research shows satisfaction comes from doing our own thing, mastering it and making progress. Engagement and autonomy is the formula for a happy, productive and loyal team. If you want your employees to be happy, empathy is the quality that makes better leaders. Pink cites companies like Google, where employees are encouraged to spend 20 per cent of their time creating their own projects. G-mail wasn't a management-led Google project but a 'free time', 'do what you like' project. Then there's open source software: created by programmers working in their own time for free and then offered for free.

What about Wikipedia? An idea launched in 2001, it now has over 34 million articles contributed by almost 23 million people, because they want to and because they can, not because they're paid. At the last count, Wikipedia had 35 paid employees.

A 'GOOD LIFE CRISIS': MARK'S STORY

Mark Williamson was in his early thirties on a fast-track career path as a management consultant when he had what he now calls a 'good life crisis' resulting in a major change in direction.

'It was like I had been running really fast up a ladder all my life, but I'd never really stopped to see whether my ladder was leaning against the right building,' he says. So he took time out to think about what he really wanted out of life – and decided he wanted to focus on making a difference to others. Since 2010, he's been director of Action for Happiness, a movement of people inspired and created by Lord Layard. Action for Happiness has a simple aim: 'Let's put the things that matter first.' Mark and his small team of volunteers help and encourage people to take personal action for a happier world. From classrooms to boardrooms to local community groups, over 100,000 people have participated so far.

Talking to Mark, I asked him how his life had changed as a result. 'I'm my own person now. I used to be very competitive, always concerned about how other people viewed me and my work. I wanted and needed their approval. Now, I know lots of people think I'm mad for doing what I do, for taking a pay cut and abandoning corporate life to run a small charity, but I don't care. I'm happier; our work is really changing people's lives for the better. That's what's important.'

Martin Seligman, one of the most respected happiness experts, helped create the whole field of 'positive psychology' in the 1990s. His book, *Authentic Happiness*, lists the three key happiness components: pure pleasure; engagement – the depth of your involvement with family, work, romance and hobbies; and meaning – using your personal strengths to serve some larger end. It turns out that pleasure is the least important of the three. As Seligman says, 'This is newsworthy because so many people build their lives around pursuing pleasure, when engagement and meaning are much more important.'

Seligman is a proper guru. The research he has conducted into happiness is legendary. In one case he asked two groups of students whether they thought happiness came more from exercising kindness than having fun. The results showed that the afterglow of 'pleasurable activity' paled completely in comparison with the effect of a 'kind action'.

He then studied the altruistic behaviour of two groups, one happy and one unhappy. He found happy people are more altruistic. When we are happy, we focus more on others than ourselves, display more empathy and reach out to share our good fortune. By contrast, when we're down, 'we become distrustful, turn inwards and focus defensively on our own needs'.

Seligman has now extended his original thinking and added relationships and accomplishment to the core list of happiness components. It sounds to me as though Seligman's findings are totally in line with Pink's research – the more we DO positive things and are actively engaged, the happier we are.

Boosting happiness

Sonja Lyubomirsky, a respected psychologist at the University of California, Riverside, found that people who take the time consciously to count their blessings every week report a significant increase in their overall satisfaction with life. Expressing gratitude and practising random acts of kindness also contribute a great deal to personal happiness.

Lyubomirsky suggests that 'these should be both random – let that harried mom go through the checkout queue before you – and systematic – take Sunday supper to an elderly neighbour. Being kind and generous to others, whether friends or strangers, triggers a cascade of positive effects. It makes you feel generous and capable, gives you a greater sense of connection and wins you smiles, approval and reciprocated kindness – all happiness boosters.'

Just saying thank you. Something that simple – preferably in person – to anyone you feel has helped you in life has been proven by Seligman to make people feel measurably happier and less depressed for a month. His tests show the impact takes three months to wear off entirely.

Lyubomirsky goes one further with the principle of counting your blessings. Just by recording three things about their day that have gone well, and why, she reports that 'people are less depressed and happier six months later'. That's an uplifting result from not even being generous to others, but being generous to yourself!

> 'Do all the good you can
> By all the means you can
> In all the ways you can
> At all the times you can
> To all the people you can
> As long as you can.'
>
> John Wesley, theologian

The secrets of happiness

During my research for links between happiness and altruism, I piled up books to skim through. But when I came to Richard Schoch's *The Secrets of Happiness*, skimming was not enough. Three hours after picking up his book, I was still totally engrossed. Schoch is a pleasure to read as he explores '3,000 years of searching for the good life' – the philosophical and religious traditions of happiness over the centuries. His book is full of wonderful common sense, such as his thoughts on caring:

We care about the integrity of our values and beliefs. We care about our accomplishments. We care about leaving a legacy to the world. We care about the well-being of the people in our lives. And, if we are being magnanimous, we care about the well-being of people not in our lives. All these cares bind us to the world – through what we believe, what we achieve and whom we love. This is the ultimately moral shape of each person's happiness and what makes it inseparable from – in truth dependent upon – the happiness of others. Happiness may and probably will begin with pleasurable feelings; but it will also go beyond them because happiness isn't really about feeling good – it's about being good. The problem is that we are apt to mistake the former for the latter.

Schoch expands this thought later in the book:

Everybody, no matter who they are, what they are like or what they do, can find happiness in a way that is right for them ... our path to happiness must begin on our doorstep, where we live; otherwise it is not ours. We do not have to forge a new life – the one we have will do just fine – nor must we wait for a more opportune moment – the right moment is always now. To be happy we must rub with the grain of our character, not against it; we must become the perfected version of the person we already are, not someone who we could never be.

'To be happy we must rub with the grain of our character', great stuff!

Those who feel good do good

'Happiness is a function of fulfilment. When people are able to express their creativity, when they have meaning and purpose in life, when they have meaningful relationships and are able to make other people happy, in general they are happy then. Focusing beyond self – happiness increases helpfulness – those who feel good do good. But doing good also makes one feel good.'

Deepak Chopra, author, doctor and spiritualist

Further endorsement that altruism and happiness go together comes from the late Christopher Peterson of the University of Michigan. His research focus was to define human strengths and virtues such as generosity. His conclusions: 'Giving makes you feel good about yourself – when you are volunteering you are distracting yourself from your own existence and that's beneficial. More fuzzily, giving puts meaning into your life. You have sense of purpose because you matter to someone else.' As Peterson says:

Being generous to another person enhances health by pushing aside negative emotions such as sadness/depression, fear/anxiety and anger/hostility. It is difficult to be angry, resentful or fearful when one is showing unselfish love towards another person.

What is the point of you?

None of these ideas are new. Abraham Maslow's 'hierarchy of needs' was first published in 1943 and he's still much quoted.

Maslow was a psychologist who organised human needs into three broad levels: physiological (food, water, a roof over your head); psychological (love, self-esteem, safety and a sense of belonging); and self-actualisation (the ability to make the best use of your talents, personality and capabilities). Self-actualisers are always striving to develop and express themselves. Once we have met our basic needs, Maslow argued, we begin wanting to be useful, to have meaning.

What we're all searching for is a sense of purpose. We are urged not to 'give up' on life. In Viktor Frankls' remarkable and powerful book *Man's Search for Meaning*, based on his personal observations of survival in a Nazi death camp, he concluded that man's search for meaning was the primary motivational force in his life. 'The meaning is unique and specific in that it must be fulfilled by him alone; only then does it achieve a significance which will satisfy his own will to meaning.'

Purpose in the death camp was linked to dignity and survival, but today we could honestly argue that purpose is about kindness, connection and generosity. Living in an unequal society, we know that a wealthier person isn't necessarily happier, and that everyone, irrespective of wealth or advantage in life, is capable of contributing to a kinder, happier world. Without it, we live in a society that is never at peace, driven by competition and profit at the expense of happiness.

Multimillion-selling management experts such as Stephen Covey also teach that a sense of purpose is a critical component to a successful life. In his book *First Things First*, written with Roger and Rebecca Merrill, Covey updates Maslow's thinking by identifying four core needs: to live, love, learn and leave a legacy. He defines them in this way:

• To **live** is to take care of our physical need for food, shelter and clothing

- To **love** is to recognise our social need to love and be loved, and to relate to others
- To **learn** is to realise our mental need to develop and grow
- To **leave a legacy** is to acknowledge our spiritual need to have a sense of purpose, personal consequence and contribution

We have to perfect the first three needs to navigate our way through life, but to experience a life truly worth living, in Covey's view, we must leave a legacy.

Every one of us is unique. We all have a great opportunity to leave the world a better place than when we arrived. We are alive for such a short while, even if we reach our eighties, and spend much of this time simply learning how to navigate through our journey of life. Working, sleeping and eating. Week by week, year by year. But we need to carve out some time to leave our own mark on the world, before our life is used up.

So how will you have used the 'gift of life'? The answer will be important to you at the end of your life, when you will inevitably have less energy to get stuck in, so it really is worth asking yourself the question now. The saying 'No one ever said on their deathbed that they wish they'd spent more time at the office' is slightly glib – but true. The deal done or missed, the salary or promotion won or lost, will not really matter.

But you *will* wish that you had spent more time with your family and friends, made up that quarrel and been more generous to others with your time and money. You will hope that you have left the world a little bit better for your presence.

Why not start right now?

A LIFE OF PURPOSE AND MEANING: JOHN'S STORY

John Sweeney, the founder and CEO of Suspended Coffees, is a charismatic Irishman with the true gift of the gab. Some of the stuff he's already been through in life would have destroyed me, but John's inspiring because he's so open and willing to share his story.

'All I have is my story. That's what people have kept on telling me and the first time I shared it publicly I was terrified.

'I was always picked on at school, bullied so badly I was nearly killed, labelled a loser, told I was stupid, that I'd no hope of getting a job; beaten by teachers and bullied so much my mum went down the legal route and my friends were told not to hang around me anymore. I'd brought shame to the family name. They went out of their way to blacklist me where I grew up in a small Irish village, though I did nothing wrong. It stopped me from ever telling my story.

'There are a couple of moments when my life changed. The latest started in October 2014; the Suspended Coffee movement I'd started got me an invitation to speak. The first time I'd ever spoken in public about anything. I'd prepared nothing and was told just before that my 20-minute slot had gone up to an hour. "Oh, and by the way, you're the only speaker and there are 85 people here." I rang my wife: "I can't do it." But she told me, "You'll be fine. You have nothing to lose."

'It was the most petrifying experience, but also the most transformational; it lit a bit of fire under me. The audience reaction was amazing – I get emotional thinking about it – they told me, "That's the most amazing story we've ever heard." And that planted a seed of doubt. Was I really such a loser? Perhaps I could achieve something and leave my mark on the world. For the first time in my life, I had a bit of self-belief.

'After school, I tried to go to college, but was always turned down. I did a bit of plumbing (I apologise now; I was no good at it) and kept on searching. On 27 March 2013 at 2.30 in the morning I was on my phone when I read the story of how Suspended Coffee worked in Italy and was immediately hooked. I felt I could have spent all my life looking for something like this – someone buying a coffee for someone else for no reason apart from being kind. There had never been anyone for me; no one had ever taken me under their wing. My motto was: "What happens, happens. Get over it."

'2.30 a.m. that day was my moment. No hesitation. *I want to start a Suspended Coffee movement.* It's when you buy your coffee, buying one extra for someone who is homeless, outside and freezing, out of work or broke; someone who'd otherwise hesitate even to come into the coffee shop. Me at various times of my life, when I'd have loved to join all those people drinking and socialising in the warmth and become, for a little while, part of that community. It's based on trust; you just leave the price of a coffee and it's up to the staff to welcome people who ask for it. A lot of our cafés give out coffees randomly as well, just to promote the power of a kind deed. And they get local groups together to share coffees and chat, because this is as much about connecting people as being kind.

'I didn't have any money to put into it, so started with a Facebook page. Along the way, I've met so many incredible people who've been kind to me and helped me get where I am. We've got over 2,000 cafés signed up officially all over the world; I reckon quadruple that doing it. Almost 300,000 "likes". The concept brightens people's day, gives inspiration for humanity. It resonates with different people in different ways and there's a team of volunteers talking to people who connect with us so they don't feel alone. We promote the idea that everyone is important and to go the extra mile. We believe in people when they are alone. For people who are a little lost, we pay it forward.

'What I've learnt most of all ... you should never wait to be who you want to be and never be afraid of it. Live a life of purpose and meaning. Live a life that's true to you. Let people who believe in you find you. You attract what you put out, so the more true and authentic you are in yourself, you will end up in the right places. You don't need to chase it, it'll come to you. Everyone I speak in front of now is ridiculously complimentary and I struggle to believe it, but then I see the smile on their face and the look of hope in their eyes and get a feeling I can't explain. Part of me is sad I never had anyone like that.

'As my grandmother says, "It's nice to be important but it's more important to be nice."'

'This is the true joy in life ... Being used by a purpose recognised by yourself as a mighty one ... Being a force of nature instead of a feverish, selfish little clod of ailments and grievances complaining that the world will not devote itself to making you happy. I am of the opinion that my life belongs to the whole community and as long as I live it is my privilege to do for it whatever I can. I want to be thoroughly used up when I die. For the harder I work the more I live. I rejoice in life for its own sake. Life is no brief candle for me. It is a sort of splendid torch which I've got to hold up for the moment, and I want to make it burn as brightly as possible before handing it on to future generations.'

George Bernard Shaw, playwright

Success to significance

Many people become successful and fulfilled in their chosen way of life, in business or industry, the arts, media, sport, teaching, as an academic or in medicine. In fact, thank goodness, in every area of life, people become experts in their chosen field of work or unpaid interests: taxi drivers, gardeners, preachers, builders, fishermen, farmers, retailers, journalists, charity workers, child-minders and computer programmers – if I haven't mentioned your world, forgive me. People work hard, succeed at many different levels and are usually rewarded in a suitable fashion. Or hopefully paid the rate for the job, at least.

But does this make their life, or yours, *significant*? This does not mean I'm suggesting giving it all up to help out in the local drug rehab unit. But I am raising the idea of living a *useful* life: recognising how fortunate you are, using your resources to help others and being worthwhile. We can all think of people we know who have either had, or who continue to have, a positive influence on our lives and of those around them. They are the significant ones, the people who leave their thumbprint on the world.

Others miss the point of life, always busy and completely caught up with their own ambitions, problems and desires. If they do help people at all, it's as an afterthought – a hastily scribbled cheque; an apology for a date missed, guiltily made up for by a present bought. When asked, of course they sponsor a friend raising funds for charity – not too much, though, as there's bound to be someone else they know asking for support soon.

This isn't a recipe for happiness.

These people never really seem to be at peace. Alain de Botton recently gently challenged them by saying, 'Next time you see someone driving a Ferrari, don't think, "This is someone who is incredibly greedy," think of them as someone who is incredibly vulnerable and in need of love; feel sympathy rather than contempt.'

Time and time again whilst researching this book I was told stories about the generosity of the poorest people on the planet. Those who seem to have so little, but gave freely to strangers because they had nothing to lose. It stands in sharp contrast to the meanness of many of those who are far more affluent, but give little for fear of losing something.

A MEETING THAT SPARKED A SHIFT IN VALUES: JULIA'S STORY

'I remember so clearly walking into a small house, built on stilts over a rubbish tip. It was the rainy season in Cambodia; the water below was full of sewage and rubbish. Mum had four kids, her husband had died of AIDS, her youngest (aged one) had AIDS and her nine-year-old daughter was a garbage picker because she didn't have the $1 a day needed for school fees. I was a charity volunteer from the UK, "doing good", visiting with a BBC journalist to get some airtime for the injustice of school fees. She sent her four kids in a tyre to come across the water to meet us. The house had one tin mug, sleeping mats, a bag of rice, a large bottle of water. Little more. Yet she was one of the most hospitable, radiant, beautiful, peaceful people I have ever met. She shared her water. That meeting sparked a shift of values – when do you really know and appreciate what you have?'

It's the thought that counts, but the action that matters

When a small child picks a flower, smiles because it's beautiful, then hands it over, you cannot help but smile too. When you ask people to recall something kind – an act of generosity – that someone has done for them recently, they always can. Often it is the small acts that both surprise and touch them. It's also one of life's rather wonderful blessings that often the less other people know of your generosity, the better you and the recipient may feel. A small act of kindness shared between just two people is truly special.

> 'Life is an echo. What you send out, comes back. What you sow, you reap. What you give, you get. What you see in others, exists in you.'
>
> Zig Ziglar, author and motivational speaker

We can never anticipate the cards we'll be dealt by life; how long we'll live, or whether a car crash or illness will change our future. The insurance industry encourages us to be cautious and prepare for the worst. We insure our houses, health and possessions. Our pets, our teeth, our future income, our pensions. But we can't insure everything. However much we might wish for long-term security, none really exists. Focusing too much on ourselves and on our futures is the antithesis of living a happy life today. In this way, a 'being' life becomes a 'having' life instead, and up go the barriers to leading the generous life we would rather live, the life that will make *today* a happy day.

If our guiding principle is survival of the fittest – always putting me, my future, my wish for a secure future first – it will be over the dead bodies of the weakest members of society. We are already living with global consumption at a level our planet cannot replenish, and global leaders are still reinforcing the message that economic growth is the key to a happy electorate.

The narrative needs to change.

The focus on looking after ourselves, our economy, our future is not something to be proud of and more and more of us are starting to ask 'Why?' We need to adapt and change and the great news is that we can and that such change is a win-win policy – because economic growth *isn't* sustainable and *isn't* linked to happiness. The Greek word '*oikos*', from which we derive the 'eco' bit of 'ecology', 'eco-friendly' and 'economy', means house or home. We are all totally dependent on one home, the planet Earth, so let's start by paying more attention to our own sphere of influence to help build the values we believe in.

By all means let's work with and support the wealth creators – but not at the expense of developing communities with the least misery and the most happiness. Make sure we tell them the importance of doing their best for the world as well as themselves. Focus on the positives. Work out your core values and live by them. Check out those initiatives that make it so easy for us to contribute: Action for Happiness, Random Acts of Kindness, Life Vest Inside, Suspended Coffees. Teach our children kindness, knowing it will make them happy. Practise positive psychology every day. Let there be less talk of bullying and more of kindness being cool. Get more out of life by putting more into it. Each one of us can show by our example that helping our fellow human beings makes us feel better about ourselves, gives us purpose and makes us happier. Each of us can reach out to people we know and lend a helping hand. Happier people are authentic people, comfortable in their own skins, nice to be around – their hearts laugh.

Develop your Generous Gene (and be happier!)

Find something good in every day. For me it's just about making time to think back over the day. Even on difficult days aim to find three good things to be thankful for, however small. A nice meal, a walk in the park, a smile from someone you love.

Use 'Acts of Kindness' cards from www.lifevestinside.com to help you with random acts of kindness. And after you've used them pass them on to spread the feel-good factor. There's a pack for kids as well.

Look for the good in everyone. Put down the urge to be critical. Why are we so negative? I'm not claiming to be permanently jolly and kind, but I feel better when I am and better when I can change a worried look to a smile. Building people up spreads happiness. It's that simple.

Be a positive parent. Of course, when people ask, our son or daughter is the most talented/bright/musical kid ever born. Whether you're a parent, teacher or simply a grown-up friend, time spent with a child, looking at life from their perspective, listening, offering empathy and support, is never wasted. Keep communicating with kids especially when they're grumpy, morose and so frustrating you want to tear your hair out. Be happy doing it, knowing this is a small investment for happiness in the years ahead.

Take time out. It may not be possible to stop whatever you're doing for five minutes every hour (if you can, brilliant), but just two minutes' meditation or mindfulness a day – quietening your mind – will make you happier, so think what five minutes could do. Get started with a free course from www.learnmeditationonline.org.

Be kind to yourself. You are enough. You are not meant to be someone else, just you. Ask for help if you're struggling, find your strengths and use them. It's your life, not your life compared to someone else's.

5

What Is Enough?

'Earth provides enough to satisfy every man's need,
but not every man's greed.'

Mahatma Gandhi

A paradigm shift to a more generous society

It's time to have a serious talk with ourselves about what is 'enough'.

We live in a consumer and capitalist society. I know that, as a consumer, I am categorised and targeted. My supermarket loyalty card gives me discounts or extra points on products they know I buy. When I shop on Amazon, the message 'People who bought this also like ...' pops up. My internet searches are tracked, analysed and sold on for pay-per-click advertisers to pop up on my home page. The holiday destination I picked at least two years ago is still being promoted to me. Hallowe'en, which involved ducking for apples in my childhood, is now massively merchandised: almost anything goes as long as it's orange and/or black. We have all been shaped by consumerism and so shouldn't be surprised that we judge ourselves and others by what we have or buy, the ingredients we cook with, being up to date with the latest fashion or food fad.

Capitalism has grown from the endeavours of creative individuals establishing businesses and developing products and services for profit. Entrepreneurs and wealth creators innovate and provide employment for the system we live in. Banks fuel global growth in part through lending for massive infrastructure projects. Politicians of all flavours woo businesses for their positive impact on the economy. I am in awe of the teenagers whose bright ideas and determination earn them millions before they reach twenty-one: dyslexic Michael Dunlop earns a six-figure annual income after he dropped out of school and founded IncomeDiary.com, which tells you how to earn money online; Farrah Gray started selling body lotion when he was six and was worth over $1.5 million by his fourteenth birthday.

Wealth equals success. We admire the people who make it and create it. We admire it for its own sake. We need the income capitalism generates for our jobs, our pensions, a booming economy ... or do we? The paradox is that capitalism in its current form is destroying forests, polluting our rivers and increasing unsustainable demand whilst we depend on our income to live the life we think we deserve.

So whilst we can start a conversation about more ethical business practices, this is also a call to change the way we live, to care more for each other and focus more on sustainability and regeneration. We are not supreme beings in control, so how can we live in a way that creates a future that works? Thinking personally – how much stuff do I need to live a happy, contented and fruitful life? Is the drive to own things really worth the sacrifice? As a world citizen, how do I feel about my use of the Earth's ultimately finite resources, from water to waste disposal? Do I care enough to change my life and influence other people?

Am I materially rich but time poor? What's that doing to my family life? Am I one of those people whose three-year-old hasn't been around me enough to know my first name? How much time do I have to connect with friends? Could there be a better, more balanced life out there?

It's important to do this assessment now, as individuals and as communities and at work, because we have officially passed the point of no return – financially, environmentally and spiritually. We cannot sustain the current trajectory without disastrous consequences. It is up to us to move society forward to one that values 'being' more than 'having' by showing others that we do; by setting out to *create* a world rather than *acquire* it; by taking only what we really need and not more than our proper share. And, yes, it's a levelling exercise. There's only enough to go round if we share what's available more widely.

The good news is that deciding what is 'enough' on a personal level is hugely liberating. It frees us from the continuous drive to accumulate things and saves a great deal of money by not buying stuff we don't really need, and a great deal of time then wondering where to put it and advertising the not-so-new stuff on eBay or storing the 'I'm sure it will come in useful someday...' stuff till we rescue it and wonder, 'Why?' Think about it, especially if you're one of the people supporting the rapidly growing UK self-storage market, now worth around £400 million a year. Storing stuff about which you'll later wonder, 'Why?'

THE FISHERMAN AND THE BANKER

An investment banker was watching the sun set over the pier of a small Mexican village as a fisherman docked his boat. Inside the boat were several large tuna. The banker complimented the fisherman on his catch and asked how long it took to catch them.

'Only a little while,' replied the fisherman.

The banker asked why he didn't stay out longer and catch more fish.

'I have more than enough to feed my family and share with our friends,' replied the fisherman.

'But what do you do with the rest of your time?'

'I sleep late, fish a little, play with my children, siesta with my wife, stroll into the village each evening where I sip wine and play guitar with my *amigos*. I have a full and busy life, *señor*.'

The banker scoffed. 'I have a Harvard MBA and I can help you. If you spent more time fishing you could buy a bigger boat. With the proceeds from that bigger boat you could buy more boats; eventually you would have a fleet of fishing boats. You would have enough fish to sell to a processing plant with no middleman involved. You might eventually open your own cannery.

'You would control the product, processing and distribution and be able to leave this small village and move to Managua. You could eventually move to New York City to run your expanding enterprise.'

'But *señor*, how long will this take?'

'Fifteen to twenty years,' replied the investment banker.

'But what then, *señor*?'

The banker laughed and said, 'That's the best part. When the time is right, you would sell your company stock to the public and become very rich. You would make millions!'

'Millions, *señor*? Then what?'

The banker sighed. 'Then you would retire, move to a small coastal fishing village where you could sleep late, fish a little, play with your kids, siesta with your wife, stroll into the village each evening where you could sip wine and play guitar with your *amigos*.'

Aren't you just a mite jealous of the fisherman and his lack of profit motive? Money saved either doesn't have to be earned at all, or can be used much more productively. 'Enough' simplifies life: everything you need, but nothing in excess.

More and more people are embarking on a personal paradigm shift, giving ourselves permission to make time for a life which has more space in it, freeing up the energy to 'sip wine and play guitar'.

At the moment we take too much. Let's take a quick look first at over-consumption of food.

Enough to eat

According to the World Food Programme, there are over 1.9 billion overweight adults in the world. Of these, about a third, over 600 million, are clinically obese. Obesity is the new epidemic. Most of us live in countries where we are more likely to die from being overweight than too thin. At the same time, about one in every nine people suffers from chronic undernourishment. Some progress has been made – the 'bottom billion' literally-starving-to-death statistic has reduced from over 900 million a few years back to an estimated 805 million people in 2014. This is a real achievement given the rising global population.

Food production isn't the issue. The world produces enough food to feed everyone. Each year, North America and Europe throw out enough food to feed the world's poor three times over, whilst elsewhere someone dies of starvation every four seconds.

Put another way, we are still, at a global level, binning about a third of all our food: scaled down to a level we can visualise, that's around 24 meals a month or almost a meal a day. Taken over a year in the UK, we're chucking out the equivalent of 86 million chickens. Every day, 24 million slices of bread end up in the bin. We're better at it than we were (a massive 21 per cent improvement between 2007 and 2014), but we still over-buy. In 2014, major UK retailers finally agreed to publish their data on in-store food waste. Tesco stats tell the story: ending up in the bin are 35 per cent of their bagged salad, 40 per cent of their apples and just under half of their bakery items. Can buying less be that hard?

Views are shifting. There's a growing lobby determined to get supermarkets to distribute food they don't sell rather than send it to landfill. In France, this has been reinforced by law. Sugar has become public enemy No. 1, linked to the growth in obesity, diabetes and tooth decay. Sugar attracts quite a bit of outrage because it's hidden away in organic, low-fat and processed products we wouldn't expect, like toothpaste and soups, as well as sauces and drinks. Full marks for taste, but zero for nutritional value – and it is addictive. Part of our survival mechanism we could well do without.

Enough. We need to eat and I know it's difficult to resist temptation and even more difficult to change a habit. If you're not on a diet or trying to manage your weight and you live in Europe, you're in the minority. So when thinking about what is enough, it makes sense to start with our attitude to food consumption and waste. Caught up in an impenetrable web of special offers, brilliant packaging and neuro-marketing schemes (so clever you can't help but buy!), we are all enticed to buy more than we need, some of which will inevitably end up in the bin. Rather than eating at mealtimes, we have become a nation of grazers and latte addicts.

John Naish observed dryly when writing about 'enough':

Girdled by multi-million-pound industries that use an ever-growing array of overt and hidden persuaders to get us to want things, work for things and buy more of them, we don't tend to complain. But if you were physically forced by powerful gangs to spend all your time and energy in the pursuit of things you didn't need, didn't want and ultimately didn't enjoy, you'd feel sorely misused.

I know I'm being programmed round the supermarket, but still find it difficult to come out with what's on my shopping list and no more. I know the bread (an 'essential') will be at the furthest point from the entrance, but the nice fresh-baked smell hits my nostrils as I walk in. Mmmm, hungry already! I know the colourful open displays of fruit and veg have been put by the entrance to slow me down with a chance to handle, select and pack. I'm a sucker for that too. When online, if what I want isn't in stock, it's oh so easy to go for the substitute.

There's a huge variety of foods we could and really should make at home. Ever thought of replacing playdough with pasta-making sessions? I guarantee most nursery-aged kids will love you for it (and you don't need to buy a pasta machine). Flour, eggs and water won't break the bank.

Over and above the 'this would be good to save time' pre-packaged fruit and veg wilting at the bottom of the fridge, I've also got too many half-empty jars of conserves, preserves, chutneys and 'sure it will come in useful one day' cans in my store cupboard to think of ways of using them, even if I spent time planning how to (which of course I don't have the time to do).

Convenience starts with baby food, for every meal of the day. We can tempt our babies with a squeeze-and-suck straight-from-the-packet puree of cherry, apple and banana breakfast, then expand his or her taste experience with a tomato-and-chicken curry lunch, followed by peaches and baby rice. Yum! And so easy for a parent on the go. Whatever happened to babies eating their parents' food mashed up?

Adults, meanwhile, have great choice if eating straight from the packet grabs you; just heat and go for some of the basics

– macaroni cheese, roast potatoes, Yorkshire pudding, rice, sausage and mash. Not to mention ... WHY are we still buying bottled water? My local supermarket has a complete aisle loaded with bottled water.

A rural African or Indian family would shake their heads in disbelief unless, as with powdered baby milk, marketing muscle had already convinced them it was better than nature.

Then there is choice. How many more reconstituted juice flavour combinations can be dreamt up? Is the world a better place for pyramid-shaped tea bags? But that's the power of a consumer economy for you. Brands need to innovate constantly to keep their market share. And the tea producer is expected to invest in the machinery to produce the pyramids without any guarantee of future sales; the salad grower to supply lettuces 365 days a year irrespective of season.

To add insult to injury, we know the content of some of our food is simply rubbish. Food manufacturers are allowed to adulterate food in a way that would have landed their medieval forebears in the stocks. Do you really want to know what goes into a pink sausage, a hotdog or a meat pie? Or cheap ice cream? How about a 'long-life' bacon brunch, with bacon, onion and potato, in a box, made in Germany – 'best before' a year and a half away? Potatoes rot. What has been done to them? What will they taste like in eighteen months? Instant cheese sauce mix has a truly sobering list of fifteen different ingredients including 'maltodextrin, dried glucose syrup, palm oil, whey powder and cheese powder (6%)' – I promise that making your own with cheese, flour, milk and butter takes only minutes.

Tristram Stuart is the author of *Waste – Uncovering the Global Food Scandal*. Stuart's book is as riveting as it is truly sobering. 'If affluent nations stopped throwing away so much food,' he writes, 'pressure on the world's remaining natural eco-systems and on the climate would be lifted ... by buying more food than we are going to eat, the industrialised world devours land and resources that could otherwise be used to feed the world's poor.'

Waste illustrates in extraordinary detail how much food is wasted by the six major UK supermarket chains from which we buy 83 per cent of our groceries and some of the reasons it happens, from deliberate over-stocking because customers like to see full shelves, to mistakenly over-stocking because the supermarket buyers predict sales inaccurately. Acres of unwanted food are simply ploughed back into the earth. Between 20 and 40 per cent of fresh fruit and veg never make it to the supermarket shelves for cosmetic reasons – too big, too small, slightly imperfect, the wrong shape, the wrong colour.

Since *Waste* was published in 2009, momentum has grown. Feeding the 5000 events (5,000 people eat a meal from ingredients saved from landfill) are happening in major cities across the UK, Europe and USA to raise awareness. There's a growing network of volunteers gleaning crops which would otherwise rot because of lack of demand. 110 tonnes (a.k.a. a million portions) were taken from UK farms in the first two years and redistributed to local charities, thus feeding some of the people struggling to feed themselves every day.

The bottom line is we KNOW all this. We just need to change. Think about the food you waste as stacks of fivers and you might sober up. Think of your health, have fun and go gleaning. There is a serious reason for getting a grip. Around a million people in the UK are regularly skipping meals because they can't afford the basics.

Enough stuff

We are a nation that loves shopping, but the Information Age is doing its bit to make us more savvy. The latest trends show shopping centres becoming 'leisure destinations', with retailers focusing on creating 'captivating' and 'inspiring' environments. We feel better buying from a company with ethical sourcing or a decent corporate social responsibility policy. Social and digital media are increasingly important. 2015 saw the launch of 'buy' buttons on Facebook, Twitter and Instagram. Bloggers chat about great new finds and find it's a profitable job. We can move seamlessly from browsing to spending. Convenience and online tools make shopping so easy we rarely have to think twice.

We quite clearly don't need all we buy. We have been persuaded to change our mobile phones on average every couple of years. And yet it follows, as certainly as night follows day, that the less we spend upgrading every aspect of our lives, from our homes to our cars to our annual holidays, the more we have left to pay off mortgages, enjoy our lives and give away to others.

As Oliver James points out in *Affluenza*, placing a high value on money, possessions, appearances (physical and social) and fame results in an obsessive, envious, keeping-up-with-the-Joneses state of mind that increases our vulnerability to emotional disorders and so becomes in part responsible for rising levels of depression, addiction, violence and anxiety. Affluenza, James believes, is the contagious disease of the middle classes. His message is 'you can choose not to do it', and he gives us a personal example:

> *There were many other changes we wanted to make to the inside of the house, having done virtually nothing to it since moving in. One day, pretty much out of the blue, the answer came to my wife: do nothing. We had a house that was easily large enough for our needs. Whilst some of it was seriously run-down (grotty-looking kitchen, dreary carpets), the truth was that we were bloody lucky to have a house at all. There were all sorts of things we wanted to do, but we needed to do*

none of them, apart from installing a new boiler (a real need in the sense that we need hot water and heating in the winter).

In the West, many of us, confronted with the simple question 'What would you like for your birthday?' find it incredibly difficult to answer. Present-giving is the social norm. No kids' party is complete without party bags to add to their clutter, rot their teeth, break within a week or quite possibly within the day. Christmas presents for sale pop up on eBay in the early hours of Christmas morning and make a post-Christmas news story. A quote on present-giving from the YouTube *Christmas in a Day* video: 'It's about you spending £100 of your money on gifts for other people that they don't want, and them spending £100 of their money on gifts that you don't want either.' Hands up those who receive presents they really don't want and at the same time give presents they suspect the recipient will not use/read/listen to. Join the club!

It is all a colossal waste of money and, crucially, *avoidable*. Think of it as a culture shift. Become a change-maker by doing very simple things. Ask for gifts from goodgifts.org and you could be buying an OAP lunch. Or resist buying a new outfit just because it's a bargain online at a 75 per cent discount. Think before you buy. Do you *really* need this?

> *Consuming has ambiguous qualities: it relieves anxiety because what one has cannot be taken away; but it also requires one to consume ever more, because previous consumption soon loses its satisfactory character. Modern consumers may identify themselves by the formula: I am what I have and what I consume.'*
>
> Erich Fromm, psychologist, *To Have or To Be?*

Simplify: get rid of stuff

Ask first: why am I buying this at all? Do I really need new clothes when my wardrobe is already stuffed full, more stuff when I already have 29 cookbooks, an apple corer, a burger press and most of the contents of a high-street chemist? Do I really need – or believe in – anti-ageing and anti-wrinkle creams, instant tan, seaweed scrubs, bath and body milks, body butter, anti-fatigue foundation 'with vitamin EFB5 and mineral-enriched formula'? Am I that gullible? Encourage the manufacturers who found that when they reduced the number of varieties of shampoo from 26 to 15, their sales went up.

Know that we respond well to a simpler life. We can close cupboard doors and find things. Over-abundant choice and the spending splurge it induces has allowed businesses to flourish, but it hasn't made us any happier.

You might like to join my fashion-conscious friend Suzannah. She sticks to a simple rule: for every new item of clothing she buys, another has to go. Buy one, take one to the charity shop. It makes her pause. It's more difficult to impulse-buy when you also need to think about the item you're going to lose. Suzannah acknowledges that it is unrealistic given our current culture not to spend anything on new stuff, but at least this has made her ask herself whether she really needs another pair of jeans. Or whether she is quite happy with the ones she has.

In a way what she is doing is simply striking out for delayed consumption. There is a persuasively argued case for delayed consumption in the US research report which uses the example of cars and the sheer material cost of making them. If you replace your car every two years and your lifetime as a driver is sixty years, you'll be the proud owner of thirty cars. Keeping your car just two years longer equals fifteen fewer cars. Keep each for six years and you'll own just ten cars – a third as many.

And we all know that with today's technology even a six-year-old car shouldn't need much maintenance.

For an alternative delayed consumption strategy, sign up to Freecycle – 'turning trash into treasure'. This is a grass-roots and entirely non-profit way of recycling what you don't want to someone who does. Perfect for when you move house or have a new baby, for when the kids have grown out of their bikes, your exercise bike is gathering dust or you've decided to learn the guitar. (Or are just fed up queuing at the dump.) It's completely free and the stuff on offer is amazing. A quick look at recent local posts found a fridge freezer, bar stool, skis, an antique wardrobe, microwave and double duvet. I mentioned Freecycle to a friend who, as a result – and with some guilt – listed a non-working PC. Yes, someone was interested. He made it quite clear that he didn't know if the PC could be salvaged and the answer surprised him. 'I'd like it for my son. He's autistic and simply loves the challenge of getting things working.' One person's clutter is another's must-have. A win-win to reduce landfill!

Since 2003, Freecycle has spread to 85 countries and over 7 million members, removing around 500 tonnes of items from landfill every day. Or in a year, just so you can imagine it, 'five times the height of Mount Everest, when stacked in garbage trucks!'

Enough time

Asset-rich, time-poor. Never enough hours in the day. Time flies. The mantras of our age. But instead of working longer hours to earn more, borrowing more to spend more, and justifying the lifestyle because of peer pressure, we can choose to focus on what is important. Remember that what makes us happy is our relationships. Knowing that we're all interconnected, let's make sure we allow enough time to build those relationships; there are few short-cuts. And that includes getting to know people we might not usually bother with. We bemoan the breakdown of society, but we are part of the problem – and consequently we do have the power to change it.

A huge number of public services, together with thousands of UK charities, work to help people in every area of life and at every stage of life. Take a moment to focus on disruptive children, kids who may struggle with or skip school, then join gangs as teenagers and too often end up with prison records.

Experts agree quality time with your children is never wasted. A baby's early experiences impact the way its brain develops. The first two years of life are crucial; an infant needs someone to give them love, attention and protection when they're little and extra demanding. Someone who is around enough to understand and interpret what they're trying to communicate and to show empathy when they're upset. Growing up, children who have developed a strong attachment to their parent/s or carer tend to be more popular with others, less aggressive, with a greater sense of who they are. They develop resilience and self-esteem. In a nutshell, children are more likely to develop into happy, healthy, independent adults when there's been someone around to give them time when they were growing up.

The same could be said of many of the adults suffering from depression, stress and anxiety. Or the loneliness and anxiety of old age. If you look closely enough at the charities that support so many vulnerable people at every stage of life and get rid of the jargon, a huge amount of what all of them do is simply give time: quality time, non-judgemental time, where someone listens, empathises and encourages. The buzzwords are 'peer support' and 'mentoring'. One-to-one long-term support, even limited to two or three hours a week, sees a marked improvement in behaviour, achievement and ability to cope with life. A single incoming phone call once a week can make more difference than you could possibly imagine.

Thousands of people put their hands up to volunteer, but family life is busy and volunteering tricky, even impossible, when both parents work (the number of working mothers in the UK has risen by a fifth over the last twenty years). So what about just making some time available for a few people whose lives cross with ours?

TIME MATTERS: JOHN AND ROBERT'S STORIES

An eleven-year-old being disruptive in class was about to be excluded. Given time to talk things through with a charity worker trained to listen, it turned out he was having problems reading and was so ashamed he'd resorted to doing a whole load of stuff (like climbing out of the window) to make sure no one found out. What he needed was a bit of extra one-to-one support to catch up with his peers, not a spell in the 'kids we've given up on' slot.

At the other extreme a senior surgeon – let's call him Robert – allocated his time between NHS and private patients. Without exception, his private patients recovered from surgery faster and Robert was pretty sure he'd discovered why. NHS patients were allocated ten minutes for a pre-op discussion, while for his private patients he allocated thirty to forty minutes. 'Most people worry before an operation, but with a little more time they understand what's going to happen in more detail and are more relaxed about it.' It was his final year before retiring, so he took a decision. 'Sod the targets. I'm going to give every patient more time.' Recovery speed improved dramatically.

Putting people before things

Belief that our self-worth depends on our material success and 'having' has left many of us feeling inadequate: in debt, hurting and insecure. Not buying things to impress in the way that we have been doing enables us to free up our enormous energies and talents to create a better and more considerate lifestyle for everyone, as well as using less of the world's resources. How much more enjoyable and productive time would you have if you spent less time shopping? Or working such long hours to earn the money to do so? Would it give you enough time to become more generous and engaged with the important issues that challenge us today?

Putting people before things will change the quality of your life, and the way you think and perceive the world will make a difference to you and an even bigger difference to other people.

A PORTFOLIO LIFE

Charles Handy is one of the world's most influential management gurus and writers, one of the first people to develop the concept of living a portfolio life, which he explains in his book *The Elephant and the Flea*. I first met him and his wife Elizabeth on New Year's Day 2004. Charles had suggested they call by on their way from London to Norfolk. The fact they had taken the trouble to meet me on New Year's Day is a clue to their lifestyle.

I was a bit in awe and had gone out of my way not to celebrate too much the previous evening to ensure a clear head! Charles is a gentle, friendly and quiet man who simply radiates wisdom. Elizabeth acts as gatekeeper to the Handy household. *The Elephant and the Flea* had intrigued me with its explanation of portfolio behaviour; a lifetime career replaced with portfolio work. In Charles's words, 'A few years ago we decided we didn't need to maximise our income; we wanted to maximise our life.'

At the start of each year, Charles and Elizabeth work out how much money they need for the year ahead. Charles adds 20 per cent because 'he worries', and then they plan how much they need to work to earn it. Elizabeth is a professional photographer. Charles could circle the world all year long, giving speeches and talks, and be well paid for it. But he would rather live a life that he enjoys than pursue wealth for wealth's sake. Sums done, the Handys then spend a third of the year working and earning, a third studying or writing and learning, and a third doing pro-bono work – helping people for nothing. They schedule 90 days for leisure.

Charles pointed out that a weekend off isn't important if you plan your life differently, and that in the right circumstances he's quite open to barter instead of payment. This began when he was asked to speak in Calcutta (en route to a paid appointment in Australia) for a very low fee. He suggested he'd be happy to waive the fee completely if his sponsor could arrange introductions and a little time in his schedule to meet three of the most interesting people in Calcutta – his sponsor's choice. The people he was introduced to included Mother Teresa, and with that he decided that asking for introductions was the way forward.

I admit to a certain amount of jealousy that the Handys have got their life so sorted! What's the point of earning more than enough when you can nourish your mind and soul by meeting some of the world's most interesting people instead? In my own small way I now try to emulate that plan. One of the principles of the Rainmaker Foundation I run is that it mixes paid work with free support. As part of my work I allocate time to search out new and inspiring charities, which hugely informs my ability to advise clients and is fascinating and often humbling. I also make time to help people out as much as I can, mentoring, advising, listening – they nearly always have the solution themselves. And that includes being there for family and friends. Nothing particularly grand or important, but all things considered, a much more balanced life.

You are probably thinking, *It's all very well for him, but ...* But you're missing the point. The important point is that when you work out what is enough for you and then do something about it, you'll be positively surprised by the improvements in your quality of life. 'Work-life blending' is the new trend. This was predicted by Handy in his book *The Age of Unreason,* written in 1989, and makes increasing sense. Commuting is time-consuming, expensive and often uncomfortable. Working from home days are now seen as normal by many employers. There's no need to take time off to wait in for the plumber. In some industries remote working is the norm. Everyone's becoming more open-minded about who goes to the sports day or parents' evening, so working parents can combine parenting with work more easily. Of course nothing beats a face-to-face meeting, but emails, Skype and sharing images can definitely reduce their number, and with this less time is spent travelling and more time living. A friend worked remotely from Paris for a week, visiting an old friend. She got loads done while he was at work and had a wonderfully refreshing week away.

For too many of us the stress of a working day comes home with us at the end of the day. Google experimented by asking their employees to leave their smartphone/laptop/iPad at work. The feedback was 'blissful, stressless evenings'. More time to chat to their partners and play with their kids, perhaps? Employers increasingly recognise the value of offering flexitime, job-sharing and part-time roles. Portfolio careers are being adopted by people in their thirties as much as those in their fifties. And if you don't feel you wish to rearrange your life so radically, do you need to stay quite so late at the office? Look at emails on holiday? Say, 'Call me any time. I'll always pick up'? Plenty of employers now actively encourage their staff to volunteer for charities; some even second employees to work with charities. Maybe you could take the initiative and cut back to a four-day week – your boss may be surprisingly receptive when he realises you'll probably do 90 per cent of the work you used to do for 80 per cent of the salary!

Enough to live on

I am often asked to define 'enough', and of course it is an impossible question: each unto their own. For a monk, a quiet place to live and to pray, simple food and some daily work; for an African villager, food, clean water, shelter and access to education and health care; for a middle-class UK parent, food, a home with enough income to pay the rent or the mortgage, heat and light, sufficient to support their children and a pension to sustain a reasonably enjoyable retirement. Almost exactly the same needs, but hugely different costs. And if, like all of us, you're a fully paid-up member of the consumer society, you probably need actively to focus on less if you're not to be carried away on the tide of more being better.

How much money do you need to live a happy, fruitful and purposeful life? Only you can decide. But answering this question will mark a turning point in your life, a small but important step in growing up and becoming useful and more generous.

More is better just isn't better anymore. Deep down, we know it is a treadmill that we need to get off – and we can choose to do so. In our materialistic society, the more we earn, the more we spend and therefore the more we wish to earn, in a never-ending spiral, totally disconnected from any concept of enough.

So, how much money do you need to live a happy and contented life? *Really* need? This is not necessarily the same as what you have programmed yourself to believe you must have. The financial freedom never to have to worry about money again ... at the expense of what?

The answer is less than you think: a roof over your head, enough food (which is not nearly as much as most of us eat), friends to support you and make you laugh, companionship, a purpose in life and very little else; though, for me, faith helps.

I can't fault the logic of the reply I got from a Yorkshire businessman when asked why he didn't expand his successful and profitable business. 'You can only sleep in one bed each night, eat three meals a day at the most and drive one car at a time.' Beyond a certain level, acquiring more things has very little practical impact on the way we live our lives each day.

'When you think, 'Now is the time to give back ...' If you're giving back, you took too much.'

Ricardo Semler, businessman and educator

Tithing – 'generosity without noise'

Tithing is the principle of giving a percentage of your income away to others, to charity or good causes. It was common in many ancient societies and cultures throughout the Middle East. It is mentioned several times in the Bible. It is a tenet of Jewish law. When I first heard about tithing, I felt it was out of order. Didn't people know that I had commitments – a mortgage, credit card debts, holidays to pay for, children's clothes to buy, school fees to survive, pension contributions to make for my old age? When I am financially stable, I will gladly give money away to others. Till then, please leave me alone.

Then, one day, I met someone who had lost his job and still gave away a percentage of what little he had to live off. I thought, if he can do it there is very little excuse for me not to, so I started very modestly, giving just 2.5 per cent of my monthly income. Shortly afterwards, I received a pay rise and, really as a sense of gratitude, it seemed quite reasonable to give a small percentage of that away as well. I began gradually to increase my monthly giving until it reached 10 per cent of my earnings. Which now includes 10 per cent of the profits of this book. This personal decision to live off less than you earn is important and will make you feel much better about yourself, especially when life is getting you down.

When a portion of your income and wealth is set aside for helping others, you won't take yourself so seriously. Putting something back into life that creates value for others as well as yourself also helps you to be thankful for what you've got, at the same time as recognising that you can quite adequately live off less. Being able mentally to draw the line at what is 'enough' is a big step in growing up, a paradigm shift.

Some argue that the principle of tithing is flawed. A person earning £200,000 who gives away or tithes 10 per cent of his or her income is giving £20,000 but still has a great deal of money to live off, save, invest or spend. Meanwhile, a person earning £10,000 a year and tithing 10 per cent is left with £9,000, which will definitely make life tougher. Added to which, once someone has mentally grasped the value of tithing 10 per cent of their income, there is a strong chance that they will hit a mental 'giving ceiling', sit back and feel pleased with themselves that they have done their bit. But those on high incomes can easily manage 10 per cent and be free to give more when need be.

If you decide to tithe, should the amount be from your gross income or your net income? This has been debated for years, but I'm afraid I rather take the view that I give away a percentage of what I actually receive, i.e. my net income. And I know that as a taxpayer the charity can claim Gift Aid and it's a tax-deductible expense for me – so worthwhile from both perspectives. Maybe I will go gross as I mature.

> *'The rich run a global system that allows them to accumulate capital and pay the lowest possible price for labour. The freedom that results applies only to them. The many simply have to work harder, in conditions that grow ever more insecure, to enrich the few. Democratic politics, which purports to enrich the many, is actually in the pocket of those bankers, media barons and other moguls who run and own everything.'*
>
> Charles Moore, journalist

Necessity versus excess

Where does necessity end and excess begin? The real enemy of enough is greed. The best definition I could find for greed was 'an excessive desire to acquire or possess more than one needs or deserves, especially with respect to material wealth'. Contrary to what the fictional character Gordon Gekko famously declared in the film *Wall Street*, greed is not good, nor right. It is ghastly. And we are increasingly outraged by it. Why should HSBC private clients be able to stash money away in Swiss bank accounts to avoid tax? Ditto companies that register offshore to avoid paying tax in the country where they operate. That they do it to increase their profits and raise their share price for those wealthy enough to be investors – and, of course, their shareholding directors as well – doesn't wash anymore.

In the boom years there was much we were prepared to tolerate, but a worldwide boom is not possible without disastrous consequences. Those in positions of power and influence need to scan the horizon beyond their bottom lines and be held accountable for the damage caused. Where is the duty of care that tries to stamp out exploitation? When Vodafone negotiates its way out of a £4 billion tax bill totally legally, at a time when the entire UK unemployment budget is £3 billion a year, all is not well. Are we comfortable with a system where the number of 'working poor' in Britain has grown to match those unemployed? Where average wages have fallen between 2008 and 2013? Where the infamous zero-hours contracts guarantee absolutely nothing to over 1.4 million 'employed'? Where some employers pay £2 an hour for apprentices desperate to work when the minimum wage is more than treble that and the living wage is £7.85 an hour, almost four times that amount? How can the drive for profit ever condone paying someone a *quarter* of what we judge they need to live? It may all make for encouraging employment statistics, but the majority of these people then need to rely on a benefits system paid for by taxpayers, whilst the commercial sector profits at their expense. So homelessness grows as tenants are evicted from rented accommodation, and shoplifting rises as benefits are cut. Is this honestly the sort of society we feel comfortable being part of?

'[Greed] is a sin directly against one's neighbour, since one man cannot over-abound in external riches without another man lacking them … it is a sin against God, just as all mortal sins, inasmuch as man condemns things eternal for the sake of temporal things.'

Thomas Aquinas, theologian and philosopher

I'm not arguing that ambition or making money is wrong. Running a business is hard work. If you succeed in making a fortune, well done. Money simply needs to be used productively and making it shouldn't exploit people who are vulnerable. For companies it is increasingly about transparency. Profit honestly, not by leaning on your weakest links. In the retail price war supermarkets can boost profits by requiring suppliers to pay for the privilege of simply having their products on the supermarket shelves. This is evidently a foolproof way of ensuring survival of the biggest and strongest at the expense of the smaller and weaker companies. And those who see themselves as our leaders need to lead by example, in my view. For instance, how come some young graduates who intern for MPs aren't even paid their travel expenses? Nothing excuses that sort of behaviour.

At a personal level, it is what we do with our excess wealth that matters. Use it wisely, focus on being significant or leaving a legacy. It is only by hoarding more than you need, or spending excessively on your self-interest, that you turn success to greedy obscenity. And the focus on 'having' rather than 'being' won't make for a happier life.

By the time the self-made Scottish-born philanthropist Andrew Carnegie died in 1919, he had given away around $350 million. Perhaps best known for his saying that 'a man who dies thus rich, dies disgraced', his philosophy had always been to share. Carnegie believed wealth was created for the common man's greater happiness and welfare, and his staff shared in his success as partners in his companies. The Americans, without the UK's feudal history of land-owning families, are still much better at giving and philanthropy than the Brits. In the USA, those who do well are expected to give generously to their local community, church, university or arts organisation. US charity patrons and trustees accept the honour and with it clearly defined require-ments for annual financial support.

The latest report on Global Giving from the UK's Charities Aid Foundation (CAF) confirms the USA as the world's leader in philanthropy when measured against helping a stranger, volunteering time and giving money. Interestingly, the US was ranked ninth when it came to the number of people giving money. Myanmar comes top. An incredible 91 per cent of the population regularly donate, which CAF suggests reflects the Buddhist teaching that giving to charity is integral to acting out your faith. More people in Northern Ireland give than from the rest of the UK.

In fact, being wealthier even seems to be a barrier to generosity, because when you have more than enough, the fear of losing it puts the brakes on. Wealthier Americans (earning over $200,000 a year) reduced their giving by 5 per cent between 2006 and 2012. The poorest (earning up to $25,000 a year) gave away 17 per cent more. It is a values thing. And it's about empathy. People living just above the breadline know what it's like below it. They embrace a philosophy and culture where you help each other out.

At the other end of the scale, let's raise a cheer for Warren Buffett and Bill Gates who broke the trend by making a public commitment to helping others when they launched the Giving Pledge in 2010. The initial list of 40 US billionaires who signed up has grown to a global figure of 138. Every one of them has pledged to give the majority of their wealth away to good causes in their lifetimes, or in their wills. As Michael Bloomberg, the billionaire behind the Bloomberg financial information empire and one of their number, said: '*If you really care about your family, it's best to do something to make the world a better place for your children and grandchildren, rather than just giving them money.*'

The hope is to inspire and encourage others to join them, but also to start conversations, learn from each other and encourage everyone, whatever their level of wealth, to do more. The Giving Pledge is a call to action.

'I've always said that there is an obscenity to money sitting on the sidelines. And I say it now. If you have the means to do something today, be a game-changer and do it. Solve a problem, animate your passion while you can still know it, feel it. It's like no other pleasure on earth.'

Dame Stephanie Shirley, IT millionaire and philanthropist

Putting it into practice

What do you want to be remembered for? The tide is turning. The 'sharing economy' is a reality for many families, friends and local communities already collaborating to create a better world. An increasing number of people are recognising the value of simplifying life and living by a different set of values. It's quite possible to work out what you need and share out the extra. To be one of the people shifting attitudes so that everyone is respected for how much they have done to help their fellow man. To experience the exhilarating power that comes when you share out your talents to change your world.

Time to ponder, perhaps, on the values and principles we are instilling in our children and grandchildren. It can be very simple to ensure you are teaching the kind of values you would like the world to follow. A friend, for example, sits down with his young family on Christmas Day for an annual ritual. The children work out which presents they will keep and which they will give away. One for me, one for someone else. On Boxing Day they visit the local hospital and offer half their presents to the kids who couldn't spend Christmas with their families. Peer pressure works both ways. The kids get a real buzz from giving their presents out and realise just how lucky they are not to be ill. They build the resilience they need to resist wanting the latest of everything. They learn to value health more than stuff.

Take a moment to think about how you can help turn the tide. It is possible, with a little thought and perhaps a dash of reason and humility, for all of us to work out our own take on 'enough'. And when you do this, you find you are somehow magically freed and more centred. You will simplify and declutter, liberating masses of excess energy to show an interest in the world.

Now to get this straight, I'm not advocating a life without treats, or one where you keep the lights switched off and retire to bed as the only warm place in the house. I'm with my fashion-conscious friend Suzannah. It is through each of us being aware and doing something positive – however small or radical – to our lifestyles that change will happen. It's about living with sharing rather than hoarding in mind.

HOW MUCH LAND DOES A MAN NEED?

In 1886, the Russian novelist Tolstoy published a short story about greed and ambition called 'How Much Land Does a Man Need?' The story goes like this.

A couple living in town debate the merits of town and country with their brother-in-law Pakhom, a small farmer living a life of honest simplicity in the country. The conversation unsettles Pakhom, who begins to think his life would be easier if he owned more land. As luck would have it, he discovers a way to get it.

A merchant passing through his village has just returned from the land of the Bashkirs, where he has bought 13,000 acres of land for 1,000 roubles. 'There is so much land that you couldn't walk round it in a year,' he tells Pakhom. 'It all belongs to the Bashkirs; the people there are as stupid as sheep, and you can get land off them for practically nothing.'

Pakhom sets off to find this magical kingdom and discovers the Bashkirs leading a very simple and happy life. He is warmly welcomed and tells them what he has heard.

Yes, there is plenty of land, their elder agrees, and Pakhom can have as much as he likes. 'At what price?' asks Pakhom. The elder replies: 'The price is 1,000 roubles a day. However much you can walk round in one day will be yours. But there is one condition. If you don't return on the same day to the spot where you started, your money is lost.'

The following morning at sunrise, Pakhom puts his 1,000 roubles into the elder's hat and sets off with a spade to mark his boundaries. After several hours he starts to tire, but keeps going. *An hour to suffer, a lifetime to live*, he thinks, and takes a detour to include a particularly good hollow where flax would grow well. Then, as he heads back to his starting point and the villagers he sees the sun begin to sink. Exhausted, he realises he has gone too far and starts to worry he will be late.

He throws off his coat, boots, flask and cap and runs towards the hill that he set off from, his heart beating like a hammer, his mouth parched and his lungs burning, and reaches it just as the sun sets. The elder is waiting, laughing. 'Ah! Fine fellow,' the elder says. 'You have gained much land!'

And with that, Pakhom's legs give way and he falls to the ground, dying of exhaustion.

Pakhom's servant digs his grave. Six feet, from his head to his heels, was all that he needed.

A practical suggestion: lifestyle offsetting

Carbon offsetting is one way we're being encouraged to compensate for the emissions we produce. Little things add up. In Kenya, gravity-fed water filters in remote villages remove the need to boil the water over an open fire, offsetting thousands of tonnes of CO2 in the atmosphere.

What we can do for carbon we can also do for excess consumerism.

So let's introduce 'Lifestyle Offsetting' as a way of compensating for over-the-top spending. When you buy something for pure indulgence, something you want but definitely don't need, offset it with a personal contribution which either builds the social capital of your local community (time spent with your elderly neighbour, offering a lift to the shops or cooking a meal) or helps someone living on a dollar a day somewhere else in the world. My guess is you won't stop buying new clothes, going to the theatre or eating out when you can't be bothered to cook – but you will think more about how lucky you are to be able to do this while millions of people around the world are isolated or starving.

I am as guilty as you. I enjoy an evening out and drink wine and I've no intention of giving up (even though I'm sure my doctor would encourage it). Life's pleasures are important! But if I tot up the amount I spend on booze and offset it in some way by contributing to an African water project, or the salary of a teacher in India, I offset my indulgences. It might mean less money spent at the off-licence next month, but that would be better for me anyway.

A LUNCH TO REMEMBER – AND OFFSET: MY STORY

I had been asked to speak at a business networking lunch. Members of the network have gathered in one of London's better-known hotels and I am introduced to several hundred people as coffee is being served. The food has been good, wine has been served and everyone seems mellow.

It's a short talk. My aim is to encourage as many people as possible to think more about helping others and to be more generous going forward. One story I use to illustrate my talk is about an amazing Indian project I visited, which feeds over 1.5 million school children a day. Chefs in huge kitchens in several cities cook through the night and deliver the meals to schools. That's important because the kids have to be at school to be fed. Just one nutritious meal a day helps stave off malnutrition, improving not only learning but also the positive life outcome of 1.5 million children. 'The cost of feeding one child a meal a day for a year is £10.'

I repeat that fact to make sure it sinks in.

'The cost of feeding one child a meal a day for a year is £10.'

Everyone in the room knows the cost of the meal they have just eaten. Everyone has paid out enough to feed a child in India for several years and consumed it in a couple of hours. There is applause, but to my frustration, little action.

A fortnight later I retell the same story to staff at Google's London HQ. Unlike the well-lunched bunch who clapped before leaving to go back to work, there was an immediate response from the Google staff. 'This is inspirational', 'What's the website?' and 'What can we do?' It takes so little to be proactive and once you've started, the next step is even easier. Big thanks to all who listened at Google and decided to act.

The charity is Akshaya Patra. Maybe the exchange rate has changed or they've made efficiencies, because Akshaya Patra's annual daily meal is now delivered for 750 rupees (£7.30). Back in 2000, its founder watched kids fighting stray dogs over scraps of food in the street and vowed to do something about it. What started as a local Bangalore charity now operates across ten Indian states, is financially supported by central and state governments and plans to feed 5 million children every day by 2020. In one fell swoop, 5 million children can develop into healthy adults; more go to school, fewer to child labour; and the education gives them a leg-up out of poverty. It's a brilliant and oh-so-simple solution.

Offsetting the cost of your meals out, especially the big ones where we tend to over-indulge, could make a real difference. And, as the penny drops, people realise it's not that difficult, it's simply a matter of doing it. Money spent on 'another frock' could become a micro-loan to help a group of women in Peru start a weaving business that will provide them with an income for life. Another pair of shoes could be left in the shop and the money used to pay for the education of a child for a whole year in Uganda. Small, conscious decisions, where you put the money you would have spent aside to create a life for others. Switch your focus to a life saved and a future created; to what you can be; to the legacy you can leave, rather than what you have. There is huge power in play when we become conscious of 'enough'. The more we realise how much we have and how little we actually need, the more generous we can be to each other.

It is tremendously difficult to change a habit, particularly one that is linked to our values and reinforced by social pressure from our nearest and dearest. But the seeds of change are already around. We turn down the heating, buy hybrid cars, install solar panels, get on our bikes, use Freecycle. If mowing or drilling isn't something you do all the time, share your lawnmower or electric drill through www.shareable.net and www.streetbank. com. Saving energy, recycling stuff and buying from charity shops doesn't mean you're broke. You're simply getting off the treadmill of 'more is better' and 'new is best' – creating a much more satisfying life and helping to level the playing field across the world at the same time.

'Enough' could be the thought that opens the door and allows the new, generous, thoughtful you to leap into action, to help others and to give. To misquote Gandhi, 'You must be the change you wish to see in *your* world.'

Develop your Generous Gene

Work out what is 'enough'. How much do you really need to live a happy and fruitful life? Do a budget, add 20 per cent, pause and ponder. The less you need, the less you have to work. Ask yourself if you **really** need a new phone/laptop/car? What would the new one do for you that the current one doesn't? Just keeping the old one for an extra year could make a big difference.

Offset your lifestyle. Next time you buy something new you want but don't need, set aside a similar sum for a homeless charity or take something you no longer wear much to a charity shop (they earn income from rags as well!). If you spend money on a meal out because you can't be bothered to cook, give to a hunger project. Or, if you drink too much, make a donation to a water-aid programme. It may not help with the hangover, but you will feel better in other ways.

Stop wasting food. Read *Waste – Uncovering the Global Food Scandal* by Tristram Stuart: your life will never be the same again. Support your local farmer's market and start buying fresh, seasonal and locally produced. Use food up rather than throw it out; eat your leftovers; use a shopping list and stick to it if you can – the thinking process alone will save you a fortune. Best of all, decide to shop at local, independent retailers rather than international chains.

Before you buy any more bottled water see http://storyofstuff. org/movies/story-of-bottled-water/

Maximise your life, not your income. Cut down the amount of time you spend at work and get a life. No one ever said on their deathbed: 'I wish I'd spent more time at the office.'

Make your own. Learn to make your own cheese sauce, don't buy the mix! Roast real potatoes, boil rice, use your blender to puree the baby food – as Barack Obama said, 'Yes, we can.' None of these things take more than a few minutes.

Buy presents people actually want. And keep a list of things you would like so others can give you something you genuinely want. Think of it as part of delayed consumption. When something breaks, live without it for a while. See if you miss it or add it to your present list. If you already have enough, ask for a gift from charities such as www.goodgifts.org where 'little good gifts' start from around £8 for a baby's blanket, a school uniform, school textbooks or even 'prize bull semen'! Bet that wouldn't otherwise make it on to your wish list ...

Tithe. Make a decision to give away a small part of your earnings each month to a good cause, local or global. Start at 2.5 per cent. Could you really not live off 97.5 per cent of your current income? You may also find that thinking through who to give it to, and the act of giving it, opens up whole new areas of interest in life.

Part 2

6

Poverty in Britain

'The poverty of our century is unlike that of any other. It is
not, as poverty was before, the result of natural scarcity,
but of a set of priorities imposed upon the rest of the
world by the rich. Consequently, the modern poor are not
pitied ... but written off as trash. The twentieth-century
consumer economy has produced the first culture for
which a beggar is a reminder of nothing.'

John Berger, Booker Prize-winning author

S o what's it like to live on the other side of the great divide
– on one of the estates up and down Britain we see documentaries about and read about but never go to? To be a
statistic that needs to be dealt with? To be on the receiving end
of austerity measures?

'Is this how we inspire young people of the future?'

DAN'S STORY

Dan knows. A no-nonsense Englishman, for over a decade he's
headed up a small charity that works with young people from
five estates. Claim to fame – the area he works in is up there
in the top 1.25 per cent of deprived areas of England. In 2004,
Dan was head-hunted to sort out a local grass-roots project

that had run out of money. 'Run out of money' being the polite way of saying 'gone bust'. Too big an overdraft, too many debts: the nightmare scenario didn't go away. But Dan doesn't give up that easily. Two donors believed in him and gave the cash to start over again.

So what's it really like? What's in the DNA of a deprived area?

'A lot of people die when they're forty-five or fifty because of their lifestyles. There's no local employment. We're now working with third-generation unemployment. When your parents don't work, it's not a way of life you even know about. We've got the highest level of youth unemployment in the country. And of course it costs, being poor. The poorest people pay the most for their gas and electric because they're on a card system. They've limited incomes so they can't buy food in bulk. They do get together to buy from Iceland because if you spend £20 it's delivered to your door. But then you've got this frozen food and the electric's cut off and the freezer stops working …

'There's a lot of conflict. It's the biggest issue when people are desperate. They ask you nicely, then threaten you and become aggressive. It's an embedded, learned behaviour which we challenge all the time. Domestic violence is part of it. J gets beaten up and her mum-in-law gets back to her saying she deserved to be slapped, happens to lots of us, just get on with it, what's so special about you? J's in a bad way so she goes to the police. That just makes matters worse because she went to the police and grassed. You don't do that. Everyone's against her now. There are lots of bizarre scenarios. Knife crime's an issue. Young people go to a party with their mates, get drunk and end up stabbing someone they know. Fights are set up to get even and everyone turns up, takes out their mobiles and films the attacks. The police cameras film them sometimes. And everyone lives on the same estate, so they don't get away from each other.

'The clampdown on benefits is hitting people hard. Particularly sanctions, because when people have done something which means they're sanctioned – perhaps turning up five minutes late for an appointment – they don't find out till they try to get their money from the Post Office and it's not there. There's no leeway. The letter arrives later.

'Less is being done face-to-face. It's "go online" or "ring the Call Centre", so you're speaking to someone in Bristol or Birmingham; someone at a distance. How would you feel if your first call is 1 hour 10 minutes on hold and ditto the next 50 minutes; so 2 hours hanging on and you've still not spoken to anyone and not got the money to pay for the next call? How would you cope if you were told your money will be in on Monday and when it's not, there's no recollection of the conversation the previous Friday? These are real examples.

'We were supporting a young woman who was about to finish a course, which meant her Income Support would be stopped and she'd move to Job Seeker's Allowance. She couldn't apply for the JSA until she'd completed the course and it would then take four to five weeks to come through. So four to five weeks with no money to get about the same amount of money on the new benefit which would then be backdated. It might make sense on paper, but over Christmas with a young kid? How's she supposed to live for five weeks? She'd come from the care system, she'd no family to fall back on, no food for Christmas and no solution. It's the small things that break people.

'It's really, really difficult but the question is: "Is this how we inspire the young people of the future?" Or are sanctions just making it incredibly difficult for people who are already downtrodden? It's not surprising that shoplifting is up. And of course it's a cash economy. If there's any work going, you're going to keep quiet about it.

'We have achieved huge things, but they take time. Some of the young people we work with are troubled, some traumatised; one girl didn't speak at all until she'd been to five or six sessions with us. She's just finished her first year at uni, even though her family were against it as they'd lose her as a carer for the younger ones. She's moved from not speaking at all to standing up and speaking out on issues she's passionate about. Some teenagers here are socially isolated. They think they're the only one stuck in their bedroom looking at a screen, but when they come here they realise there are others like them and it's great to see them support each other and learn from each other. Their creativity and the inspirational things they do are heart-warming.

'We look a lot at actions and consequences and the young people came up with discussion cards. What are the pros and cons of using knives? A five-year sentence? When this actually happened, we kept in touch with the lad in prison as well as the lad on the estate. We asked: "How did you feel being arrested? What will you do when you bump into the lad who knifed you when you're out? What will he do when he bumps into you?" When he'd been out two days they met, had a conversation and shook hands; they'd moved on. A great result.

'When we first arrived, about 60 kids were causing havoc, out of control, smashing things, stealing motorbikes, being pressurised by the police for vehicle crimes. So we worked with them to identify the issues and solve them. They need the speed; let's find a legal way of doing it. The go-kart project needed £16k to get off the ground and it's still going. We've next to no problems with vehicles now. There's been a strong urban art culture around since the 1980s – graffiti and tagging. So we identified two street spaces where street art could be encouraged and last year there were over 500 artworks there and very few anywhere else. The young people have created informal education packs and resources on domestic abuse, self-harm, alcohol and legal highs. They use real-life stories as case studies and pull no punches. The packs are being piloted in schools at the moment and other boroughs are interested in using them. Everyone is totally stoked up that we can do this.

'One amazing story is Joe's. He lives on the edge of the estate and was poorly from birth, till he had a successful heart transplant when he was fifteen. He wanted my help to do something positive about organ donation and was asked to sing at a celebration event for donor families. As he told them about how it felt to be a recipient and publicly thanked the donor family for his heart, he had at least half the room in tears. The donor family, by total coincidence, was in the audience and asked to be introduced. They met and looked at one another. "Do you mind if I feel my son's heart beating in you? That's so brilliant that my son's heart is in you. Live life, give life." I was welling up as he told me. I still well up now. And Joe's a creative guy determined to do his bit, so we've taken an idea he had and found someone to fund five different great big organ costumes which people can get into, and we're planning a flash mob in the park, a stand-up comedian and a whole lot of dialogue, so the lungs and the heart will be arguing about things like having a fag, and someone with a heart transplant will be talking about the great new life he's got.

'Employers can take advantage. People who want to work are caught in the poverty trap. A lad's really excited as he's got a job selling TV packages door-to-door, 100-per-cent commission. It's a forty-minute bus journey to the area he's been given and he needs to pay his own travel expenses from day one. Another company doing factory work puts new people on faulty machinery, with no cooling fans. They start to feel ill after a few weeks, but take a day off and there's no pay. Or as they're on probation, they get sacked with no pay after they've worked 20 hours. The next recruit will last no longer.

'Other local businesses are brilliant. One set up a food bank and one of the lads came to me with a thank-you card. I gave it to the MD and thought nothing of it. Six months later the MD got in touch and said he wanted to help that lad out. He was a decorator who'd not worked for six years. He felt low and depressed – a nobody. The MD had a maintenance job going, but the lad would need to pass his driving test to drive the van. We funded him to do that, he passed first time and two years later the feedback is great. He's exemplary, has a smile on his face every day, he can't do enough. And I know his life has totally turned round. The MD was very kind. Why did he bother? He told me he was under a lot of pressure at work at the time and offering to help the lad out helped him feel better about his own life. Every time he saw his new maintenance man he knew his actions had actually boosted him and helped him get through that rough patch. The MD felt better.'

Dan's stories aren't isolated incidents, but replicated across the country. A cross-party parliamentary committee concluded that the current benefits-sanctions system 'is unfair, excessively punitive and does little to help people get into work'. Of course sanctions hit the weakest members of society hardest. Numerous bodies have researched the impact and illustrated their reports with cases. What follows is an extract from a report by Sheffield Citizens Advice: 'Alan is single, fifty-five, and lives with his mum in a council house. He has learning difficulties and is dyslexic. He has no formal qualifications and attended a "special school". He was sanctioned for not actively seeking work. When, with the help of Citizens Advice and after a delay of six weeks, the sanction decision was overturned following "mandatory reconsideration", the decision-maker said there was: "No information on our client's case file to indicate that he had any disabilities or problems with literacy."' This for someone who was unable to read or understand any correspondence without one-to-one support.

Sanctions don't seem to be the last resort the government suggests either; some Jobcentre advisors are being encouraged to maximise sanctions (after all, those sanctioned don't appear in the unemployment stats *and* reduce the benefits bill) – Angela Neville even resigned from her job as a Jobcentre advisor to write a play about it: 'I didn't like getting brownie points for cruelty.' Benefits claimants are being instructed to live off thin air until their appeals are heard. How can they possibly do that? The assumption is that claimants are work-shy and want to play the system, but there's no evidence that's true for the vast majority. Little wonder applications to food banks grow day by day.

So it's up to us to support Dan with his team of just two, Julie and Rob, and people like them across the country. They're inspired by the young people they work with and I am definitely inspired by them. Last year, this run-on-a-shoestring charity involved almost 400 young people by running courses, organising visits to the seaside (often the participants' first ever) and canoeing trips, paying for interview outfits, creating mosaics and spray-paint art, building self-esteem, connecting with elderly locals to help with shopping – and much, much more. It's anything but easy, but when you know a bit of the detail, it seems Dan and company are solving some fundamental problems the policy-makers struggle with. Building people up, not knocking them down. This is not broad-brush stuff, it's detailed one-to-one work that's simple but effective. It's long term and works with different people in different ways. All the work costs around £150,000 a year: an average of £3 for each individual session provided. The cost to keep one person locked up for the same time averages about £35,000 before court and policing costs. I can't start to imagine the police time that would be needed to investigate joyriders and stolen bikes, or the council resources involved in cleaning up graffiti adorning local walls. And what price an estate people are proud to be part of? Last year three young people went to uni from families with three generations of unemployment, and fifteen found jobs. That's a big deal.

These are small numbers ... until you remember the ripple effect. It doesn't really matter whether we are the fifth, seventh or tenth richest nation in the world. All it takes is for us to get to know people as people, not as shoplifters or scroungers; to understand and reach out a hand of friendship, an introduction, some interview training: a gesture often worth a hundred times more than a shedload of money.

We all need to get out more

So why aren't we doing all this already? Part of the problem is that we exist in circles of 'people like us'. If you've had a decent education and not ended up on benefits you may feel broke, but you can hold your head up and live in the UK with a roof over your head and enough food to keep body and soul together. Even then, life can increasingly feel uncertain and risky. There's no such thing as a job for life anymore. We are adapting to fixed-term contracts, zero-hours contracts and more. Few of us know with any certainty what the future holds.

I still hear people insist that 'real poverty' doesn't exist in Britain, and I have to say it's a remark guaranteed to raise my blood pressure. 'Not like the terrible poverty in Africa where people face starvation and possible death from starvation every day.' And of course while the world can be divided into rich and poor nations, money seems to go further abroad. The point I'm trying to get across is that poverty in the UK is real and right on our doorsteps. And because it is *here*, it *is* within our power to look after our own, we just have to choose to do it.

We somehow see the poor in Britain as different and all too often write them off as trash. 'It's their fault for being lazy'; 'The kids just bunk off school and the parents don't care'; 'They spend all their money on fags and lottery tickets'. Think of poverty in Britain and many people think of dysfunctional families on benefits who are simply irresponsible. The feeling is they don't deserve our compassion. Being poor is seen as *their* fault. We're not a drought-stricken warzone.

The trouble is it's only when you get to grips with the work that people like Dan are doing that you begin to get the reality. Kids growing up alone in their rooms, totally socially isolated because there is nothing to do and no money to do it anyway. Adults who can't beat the system and a system that has the power to push them over the edge. Suicides linked to withdrawal of benefits. Six people a day dying after having their disability benefits stopped because they're allegedly 'fit for work'. There are no established links between the stats and cause of death say the DWP, but it seems rhetorical to ask: why are people dying if they're fit? It's a system that's so over-stretched people often have to fight to make it work for them. That's the reality.

Trickle-down economics – the idea that wealth trickles down to everyone else, so we're all better off – hasn't happened. The UK economy has more than doubled since Margaret Thatcher was prime minister. And the number of impoverished households has more than doubled too.

One of the insights that comes from working in the charity sector is that the bureaucracy and government systems we live with make services difficult to deliver. The world of civil servants is one accountable to the current minister, who is intent on delivering manifesto promises before the media starts flinging accusations of failure. Bureaucracy is thriving: 'evidence', 'consultation' and 'case histories' support or challenge statistics upon statistics. Decisions cannot be made lightly for the media will tear them apart (so what's new? They'll likely tear them apart anyway). To civil servants' credit, when time allows there is a desire to understand 'real people', even if it's only to discover a soundbite or a photo opportunity. 'We need to know what works, we need to know how to get through to hard-to-reach minorities,' the ministers and civil servants say. 'Well,' charities reply, 'listen to the people who are doing it.' Often, understanding dawns only when a civil servant has time to leave the mountain of office paperwork and talk to a child at a primary school who's never eaten a piece of fresh fruit in her life (think food deserts, transport costs, a low household income and no fridge). But even after understanding, there is another hurdle: 'We need to get public opinion on our side.'

I'm not pretending their job is easy (senior civil servants tend to be a bright bunch) but success politically and bureaucratically seems linked to not rocking the boat too much and creating a statistic to prove the problem's being tackled and the people affected reduced. Charities who know the reality are always nearer the coalface. People's lives are messy; there's no 'one size fits all'. When I asked a civil-service contact, 'What does this [hugely unjust] issue mean to you?' the answer was, 'It pays my mortgage.' Full marks for honesty, but unsurprising then that we have created a system based on targets and outputs and data, and that we prioritise that over understanding the less measurable messiness that is so many people's lives. As night follows day, the most vulnerable – those who don't understand how it all works – suffer most.

The answer is, more than ever before, in our hands, because we can get to know people as people, not statistics. We can be self-centred or other-centred. It is our lack of knowledge of and sheer callousness towards those whose lives are such a struggle that has always angered me. This is not generous; it is intolerant, arrogant and selfish. But then, I was probably heading there before I had the good fortune to meet Sammy, create a charity for disabled children and gain an insight into their utterly heroic lives and the wonderful, unquantifiable love of their families. I guess what I'm trying to say is that it's within everyone's power to create a better quality of life in Britain, because it's about reaching out non-judgementally to those around you by whatever means you can. You just need to get out of your comfort zone from time to time and discover what's really going on.

The inconvenient truth

'It would be nice if the poor were to get even half of the money that is spent in studying them.'

Bill Vaughan, author

Numerous respected organisations spend thousands of hours and millions of pounds measuring poverty levels in the sixth biggest economy in the world – yes, right here in the UK. There's 'absolute poverty', 'relative poverty', 'the working poor', 'adults in poverty'... Think of a group and you'll likely find a debated statistic for it.

Overall about 13 million people in the UK live in poverty, roughly 20 per cent of the population. That's poverty defined as a household income that's less than 60 per cent of the average (median) income after housing costs. Over 10 million fall into the 'absolute poverty' category (severe deprivation of basic human needs) with the trend still upwards. The larger number includes 'relative poverty' for people who can't afford to live a 'normal life'. They don't have enough money to put food on the table, keep warm or do everyday things like visit friends and family.

When the oven blows up or a window gets broken, there is nothing to cook with and the rain comes in. Many skimp on food for themselves to feed their children. Health inevitably suffers. Putting up with a damp, mouldy, privately rented flat with dodgy electrics is commonplace and when you complain, you know what you can do: stop complaining or get evicted. Evictions are now one of the main causes of homelessness. I wonder who chooses to place you as someone in the 'relative' or 'absolute' slot. I'm sure there's a science behind it, but I'm willing to bet 'relative poverty' feels 'absolute' when you're living it.

Put our prejudices to one side here. Very little of this is happening because people are work-shy – one in every six adults in poor households form the 'working poor', with almost half working 40-hour weeks. But average wages have dropped in real terms between 2008 and 2013, while fuel costs have soared.

Despite the efforts of successive governments, the policies to reduce poverty have consistently failed our most vulnerable. Real people living out their lives, just trying to cope, have been failed. Poverty is a root cause of violence, drug use and gang culture as a way out of a life that doesn't seem worth living. Poverty has associated exported costs borne by society as a whole; the mental and physical manifestations of poverty cost the NHS billions each year, whilst the lost potential of poor children represents lost economic possibilities for the UK. In sum, the existence of poverty costs us all: financially, socially and economically. It's very far from a world where what matters most is to create caring societies with the greatest happiness and the least misery.

In one sense, the naysayers are right. Relative poverty in Britain isn't anything like the desperate poverty experienced by the bottom billion – it's just, as it says, relative to what most of us would see as a normal life, where we can make ends meet, feed the kids and ourselves. It is still, nevertheless, real poverty – and it is deeply shocking that in a supposedly civilised and wealthy Western country, one of the richest in the world, millions struggle to find somewhere to live, consistently juggle bills and debt and depend on food banks to keep going.

CALL YOURSELF POOR: THIYWE'S STORY

I was touched by a conversation I had with a Zimbabwean refugee and friend, now living in London. 'When I was living in Zimbabwe,' she said, 'we never thought of ourselves as poor. We were all in the same boat, families and friends together, getting on with life.

'In London it is different. Here I am poor. I need money for the bus, money to visit friends. My family in Zimbabwe don't understand. They think I have a place to live, I have clothes, I have food. How can I say I feel poor? But I am.'

Winter is coming

Here's a statistic for you: '31,000 excess winter deaths in England and Wales last winter,' says Age UK. If winter lasts for a generous six months, this means someone died of cold or of the complications from being cold every 10 minutes; most of these people were over the age of seventy-five. Age UK also points out that, even when you make it through the winter, elderly people living in under-heated homes are more susceptible to respiratory and heart problems, infections and depression. All this at an estimated cost to the NHS of well over £1 billion. The winter of 2015 meanwhile is anticipated to spike to 'over 40,000 excess winter deaths'. Shall I jog your memory? Over seventy-fives are the fastest-growing demographic in the country, with numbers expected to double in the next thirty years. One day, not far from now, you and I will be amongst them.

We all know fuel prices have soared, but the reality is, if you depend on a state pension, it's often a case of choosing to eat less in order to stay warm. The official advice is to eat well *and* stay warm, as well as to improve the energy efficiency of your home (something that elderly people may not prioritise if they don't think they'll be around for long). But when the purse strings are tight, many people simply can't do both. It's eat or heat – you decide.

So next winter, think about inviting your elderly neighbour round for a cup of tea or a bite to eat. You could be helping to save their life. Not something people usually think about.

Rise of the food banks

We're a nation with over a million people using food banks. Record numbers arrived for three-day emergency rations at centres run by the Trussell Trust in the twelve months to April 2015: 19 per cent more than the previous year. It's worth remembering that no one can just turn up at a food bank, you need to be referred by a social worker, doctor or care professional first. Trussell Trust runs over 400 centres with support from local communities. Five years ago, they had under 100. So why, as the economy recovers, are more and more people not able to make ends meet in this wealthy nation?

Trussell have been doing this for a while and understand why people come. The main drivers are low wages, insecure work, benefit delays and sanctions and debt. They know as well that many are too proud to go to a food bank and will struggle on if they can. And of course Trussell aren't the only food provider. FareShare takes surplus supermarket food and redistributes it to almost 2,000 local charities and community groups. Breakfast clubs for kids, food for homeless shelters and social clubs for the elderly. Another 15 million meals provided.

Every single day of the year, in towns and cities throughout Britain, excess food is being dumped in enormous quantities whilst people in the same communities struggle to feed themselves. More is being redistributed, but you might want to question anyone who works in the food manufacturing and processing business, or the manager of your local supermarket and ask how they feel about this. Having demanded the perfect apple and the straight carrot, we've ended up with produce at prices that a whole load of people can't afford, so it takes charities to step in and make sure the most vulnerable citizens of this wealthy nation don't become a burden on the NHS because of malnutrition.

How to work flat out and still be broke

JOB = Just Over Broke, as the saying goes. This one needs revisiting. Half of the people we classify as poor are working *and* broke. Dr Vincent Pattison is one of the country's leading experts on UK poverty and works at the Ingeus Centre for Policy and Research. He was one of the first to identify working poverty as the 'hidden' poverty in the UK, way before it was hitting the headlines. This is what Dr Pattison says:

> These households are not the usual suspects in the public's perceptions of 'the poor' and cannot be readily dismissed as work-shy, feckless, lazy, undeserving or any of the other negative discourses of 'the poor' in the UK.
>
> All the major parties agree that work is a sustainable route out of poverty. However, I would argue that only sustainable

work is a route out of poverty; i.e. decent work with career development opportunities. Unfortunately, due to market-based deregulation of UK labour and labour relations, too many households (remember, the majority of poor house-holds in the UK have at least one member in work) become trapped in low-paid work. For too many, entry-level work has no exit strategy.

The summer 2015 budget announced an increased living wage 'to make work pay'. The cost of the increase in the living wage is estimated at £4 billion; the scheduled cuts to the welfare budget £12 billion. As the Institute for Fiscal Studies points out, to suggest people on welfare will be better off is arith-metically impossible. For me, this gives a motivation beyond the desire to create a society 'with the most happiness and the least misery'. I want a society where any employer offering a non-living wage and making a profit is lobbied and ostracised till they change their terms for employees. A society where we inspire and encourage people struggling to make ends meet rather than accept the culture of Jobcentres with targets for benefit sanctions.

Let's remind ourselves of the reality. Comparing the 1990s to 2012, there are 3 million more people living in inadequate housing, and double the number of people who can't afford to heat their homes. More people are living their day-to-day lives with cold and hunger than ever before, and many of them *are* working. We all know that policy-makers deal in statistics so it is up to us, as individuals, to think about the stories behind the numbers and connect. Local initiatives mostly operate from hand to mouth and you will find them all over the country. If you're an employer, connect and see how you might help. If you don't see how you personally can help, connect and ask.

HOW DO YOU PUT A VALUE ON CLEANING A HOSPITAL?
DEBBIE'S STORY

Dr Pattison cites Debbie as an example of someone whose work keeps her poor. Debbie is an outsourced cleaner at Wythenshawe Hospital, working for a multi-national corporation contracted to provide 'soft services', such as cleaning and portering. The arrangement is part of a 35-year Private Finance Initiative (PFI) agreement.

Debbie's job is to clean 110 bedrooms and several communal areas and corridors in six hours. She has her own designated area as one of a four-woman cleaning team. All four women work the same hours, doing the same job, wearing the same uniform and sharing the same cleaning materials, but Debbie is paid less. What makes Debbie's situation different is that she is the only employee in her team who started after the private company took over. So she isn't protected by TUPE (the acronym for Transfer of Undertakings (Protection of Employment)). And as well as being paid less, she also isn't entitled to any sick pay and is given fewer holidays than the three ladies who were previously paid by the NHS. The reason? Their original employment terms and conditions are guaranteed under TUPE.

Put yourself in the private company's shoes. I'd guess it was a competitive tender and price played a significant part in winning the contract. The principle cost of any cleaning contract is staff, so the only way to improve profitability is to squeeze the terms and conditions where you can and demand more work from the existing teams. This might begin by not replacing staff who leave or are off sick. It continues with new terms for new employees which are not as generous as the original contracts they had previously agreed to honour. And in truth, the private company is doing only what everyone else in the industry does. As night follows day, this is the inevitable knock-on effect on some of our lowest-paid workers when public services are outsourced to the private sector. It is the front-line staff, such as Debbie, who bear the brunt of the new, 'more efficient' delivery model.

Now let's look at it from Debbie's perspective. Her work is dirty, hard and very important for both the patients' health and the smooth running of the hospital, but cleaning is also an unskilled, low-paid job. Labour economics tell us that wages represent the productive value of one's work and so people are highly paid because their work is deemed to have high value to the economy. Those on low pay have little productive value. With that in mind, how do you put a value on cleaning a hospital?

Debbie is paid 53p an hour above the minimum wage, but even though she works full shifts and lives with her mum and three siblings at home, after rent, bills and transport she struggles to buy enough food every week. She buys economy brands and relies on things that fill her up rather than anything more healthy and nutritious. She rarely socialises. She gave up her one and only social outlet – playing football – because she could not afford the travel and match fees.

Debbie takes pride in her work and feels she should at least receive the same terms as the rest of her team. With a little more money, she could afford better food, a social life or some new clothes. However, these basic requirements in twenty-first-century Britain are out of her reach. Home is a poorly insulated three-bedroom house. Her two younger sisters (aged fourteen and eight) share a bed in the room where she also sleeps. Moving out isn't an option – she can't afford it and her family can't afford for her to move out either because of the money she is bringing in.

You can say Debbie should have known better or tried harder, but let's briefly consider her life to date. Her mum used to work at the hospital too, but is now on long-term sick leave due to a bad back (all too common in this type of work) and depression (brought on by a life in poverty and a low-paid, dead-end job), so Debbie is now the main breadwinner. She wanted to stay at school and go to university, but has worked since she was sixteen to put some money into the household. One of her best routes out of poverty ended there and then. She is now in a low-paid job with no prospect of escaping from this end of the labour market. Like her mum, she has already had considerable periods of time off work due to stress and depression. Unlike her mum, she has never had any sick pay.

The most poignant thing about Debbie is that almost any one of us could have ended up in her position if our lives had taken a slightly different turn.

Child poverty

Possibly nothing defines the true values of a society more than the way in which it treats its children and young people. How it teaches them values such as kindness, compassion and generosity as much as maths and history. How it teaches the importance of service, contribution and respect as much as the importance of getting on in life. And how it cares for them.

How do kids in the UK fare today? As you'd expect, where there are poor families, the kids suffer as well. Nutritionally, academically, healthwise. In 1999 Tony Blair pledged to halve child poverty by 2010 and eliminate it by 2020. In 2010 there was a Child Poverty Act and the End Child Poverty Action Group signed up over 150 charities. It doesn't bear to think about the investment made to co-ordinate meetings and lobbying, to build an over-arching website for 150 different organisations: think of the days spent delving into statistics, commissioning research, putting the website together, publishing findings. Added to that, we have government-appointed Children's Commissioners for England, Scotland, Northern Ireland and Wales. Everyone agrees. We don't want to be a country where millions of children don't get enough to eat. We don't want to live in a world where kids' whole lives will be affected by impoverished childhoods.

So is all this effort working? The Institute for Fiscal Studies did a report in 2011 to find out. Said report included lots of analysis about the changing levels of relative and absolute poverty, and concluded only that the target has always been 'extremely challenging'.

Save the Children issued another report in 2014. To quote: 'Our political class is sleepwalking towards the highest levels of child poverty since records began while promising to eradicate it completely.' They project that by 2020, 5 million children will grow up trapped in poverty; an increase of 1.4 million from 2015. When people can't find work, and there's no food and the bailiffs are at the door, the children suffer most.

The UK used to hold the dubious honour of being the worst industrialised country to grow up in as a child. In the light of the economic turmoil of 2015, Greece has now taken our slot.

SUCCESS IS SOMETIMES KEEPING A CHILD ALIVE: WENDY'S STORY

Primary school is many children's first glimpse of a world outside their home. It's their first real opportunity to learn how to mix with other kids, to begin to cope with life, to play, add up and subtract, to read. Here, tomorrow's people are being made: future mums and dads, tradesmen and women, entre-preneurs, career politicians, businessmen and women.

On this occasion, I have travelled to the north-west of the UK, encouraged to visit a primary school whose inspirational head teacher, Wendy, is working on the front-line of modern-day education. I am visiting a town which rose to prosperity during the industrial revolution, but where the traditional employment base has been in decline for decades. It is now one of the poorest towns in Britain, in the top 6 per cent of the most deprived boroughs. The percentage of its working-age population claiming Employment and Support Allowance (ESA) is 13 per cent, almost double the national average.

Unsurprisingly, local educational achievement reflects these economic disadvantages and the town's educational track record is abysmal. Three of the five secondary schools are in the bottom 5 per cent of the national league tables for added value between the end of Key Stage 2 and the end of Key Stage 4, and two are in special measures. Meanwhile, in the centre of town, 15 per cent of properties are empty and 27 per cent classified as unfit to live in. Four in ten households rely on some form of state benefit. Poverty is a serious problem, as are ill health, drug and alcohol misuse, depression, domestic violence and crime.

The primary school I am visiting is modern, the result of a merger between four smaller primary schools. It is bright, warm and bustling, with 300 noisy boys and girls aged from three to eleven and an equally energetic, mostly young, teaching staff of sixteen, led by a remarkably warm and enthusiastic head called Wendy. She knows everyone by name and gives all the outward signs of being powered by several Duracell batteries.

At first sight all looks good and well, but this school has the dubious cachet of being one of the 'most challenging schools in Britain'. Its catchment area comprises neighbour-hoods that almost all fall into the bottom 5 per cent in terms of socio-economic indicators. Most parents are on benefits. The surrounding housing is poor. Half the homes are boarded up and shops are scarce.

Wendy tells me the majority of children come from single-parent families. Sixty-eight per cent are eligible for free school meals. A significant majority arrive having experienced some kind of emotional trauma. Many witness domestic violence; most come from families with alcohol- or drug-related problems; many have parents with mental health issues. I am not using 'many' and 'most' lightly. This is a fact. And parental background is critical: by the time these children are five years old, they will have spent more hours with their parents than they will spend at school throughout their entire education.

Of the 150 families represented at the school, 12 are known to be in work. Third-generation unemployment is common, which means there is no history or memory of work whatsoever in many of the families. As Wendy walks me round the school and I talk to some of the kids I realise employment isn't an aspiration because the kids have no reference point. 'What do you want to be when you grow up?' I ask. 'A man.' 'When you're a man, what do you think you'll do?' 'Go down the post [office] … where the benefit money is paid out.' Job done.

Given their backgrounds, it is a miracle that many of the children make it to school each day at all. But, for the children, going to school has some advantages, even if the purpose isn't always clear – nor is it always for the education they'll receive there. School is warm, they get breakfast and lunch, some of their friends are there, and a couple of the teachers are magic and huggable.

And while the teachers themselves join up to teach, they can't operate here unless they know each child and their family circumstances well. They must learn that the real reason one child is not at school every day is because her mother is clinically depressed and can't get out of bed to bring her in.

Another's aggression is learned from witnessing domestic violence at home on a regular basis. When I visited the school, the Child Learning Mentor – the key person who works to resolve the family issues that affect the children – had been off work for six weeks with stress; probably because ten people doing that job would still not have been enough.

Wendy introduces me to a boy of nine who lives with his mum and two younger siblings, aged three and six months old. Mum was fourteen when he was born and struggles with post-natal depression. She is unable to cope with his behaviour at home, is violent, bullies her other children, hates the boy and regularly threatens to put him into care.

Another child has been excluded twice after assaulting a teacher. His mum has both overdosed and attempted suicide by hanging. After the latter, she was admitted to A&E but discharged herself with the drip still in her arm.

I am reeling in the knowledge that is the life experience for many of these 300 children on a daily and weekly basis. Their reality; what they know. Their peer group will shape their life and their expectation, in a similar manner to prisoners, who learn all they wish to about crime by being locked up together. There is a desperate shortage of positive and inspiring role models, and only occasional flashes of hope of escape into a better universe. If you spend a few hours amongst these children, and then press an imaginary fast-forward button, it is very difficult to arrive at an optimistic, happy ending. In ten years' time, these very small people will have survived their education and one or two may have landed on their feet. By then we may also be debating what to do with the fourth generation of unemployed who, finding themselves deserted by cutbacks and sanctions 'at the post', will only ever travel outside their neighbourhood to visit the nearest cash machine. Living lives that are totally out of sight and out of mind.

When I asked Wendy what she saw as success, she thought for a moment and then, in all seriousness, replied that in some cases success was the fact that the child was still alive. And then she went on to relate the story of the starfish.

The story of the starfish

A man was walking along a beach. The sun was shining and it was a beautiful day. In the distance he could see a young boy going back and forth between the surf's edge and the beach. Then he noticed hundreds of starfish stranded on the sand. The boy was hurling them one by one back into the sea.

The man was struck by the apparent futility of the task. There were far too many starfish to save. But, as he approached, the boy continued picking up starfish one by one and throwing them into the surf.

'You must be crazy,' said the man when he reached him. 'There are miles and miles of beach covered with starfish. You can't possibly make a difference.' The boy held the man's gaze. Then he stooped down, picked up one more starfish and threw it back into the ocean. He turned back to the man and smiled. 'I made a difference to that one!'

UNICEF monitor child poverty across the industrialised world and their latest (2014) report confirms what we know intuitively: children suffer disproportionately. Even the best parents find it impossible to hide lack of food, worn-out clothes and family tensions. Take a moment to think what being evicted feels like to a child. UNICEF suggests that 'the impact of the recession on children will be felt long after the recession itself is declared to be over'.

So child poverty is rising – has risen in the UK since 2008 and is on an upward trend, expected to continue *at least* until

2020. This is not something that happens just in 'the North' or in areas of extreme deprivation. Look around and you will find similar scenarios in any town or city from London to Liverpool, Norwich to Newport or Nairn.

In many ways, and without exaggeration, the lives these children live are on a par with those of the street children of Delhi. Each day is a survival course.

Make a difference

To many, 13 million people in poverty seems too big a problem to solve. That figure includes one in every three children, by whom the future of this country will be shaped. When I mention these statistics, I usually get an embarrassed silence or a blank stare in return; there are too many starfish. Of course figures induce stupor. The figure of 13 million seems to put the issue well beyond our grasp and its large-scale anonymity reinforces the stereotypes of gangs, pregnant teenagers, chaotic adults and the benefits-scrounging unemployed. It makes it something only the government can tackle (but which successive governments have clearly failed to tackle), whilst we sit back in the cosiness of a warm living room before sleeping soundly in our own comfy bed, because we believe there's little we can do.

But my message to you is that we can make a difference – even if it's just to one starfish, one person, at a time. So I will support a *Big Issue* vendor, or someone who comes to my door selling sponges, torches and tea towels. I go out of my way to talk to someone homeless on the street. I see them and do my tiny bit because they've entered into my space. If we are to move from passivity to action, we need to be brave enough to get out more and experience first-hand what's going on. To move from being the largely passive recipients of edited TV and press highlights that don't intrude too much, to being participants in a place which is more thought-provoking and uncomfortable. Even if you work full time, you need only invest a day, maybe less, to check out how the other half lives.

Every politician must be aware of what's going on and the impact it is having on our schools and indeed on our society and its future prosperity and happiness. All media editors must know it too. But somehow we as individuals and as a society fail to relate. It's a story we're distanced from. It's not up to *us*, surely, but *them*. It is a national scandal almost on a par with Dickensian times; only now there is no Dickens to draw our attention to the poor and the workhouse.

For those of you who believe that charity should begin at home – here is your chance.

Develop your Generous Gene

Learn as much as you can about poverty first-hand. Begin to see people as decent people trying hard, not as statistics. For city dwellers it will be easy and you will be shocked. There will be real poverty and hardship within half a mile or a mile of where you live. Just look. Rural poverty is more hidden, but you don't have to dig too deep to find it.

Listen. Practise empathy before judgement. Many people get very tough breaks in life. Redundancy can quickly lead to relationships breaking down and homes breaking up. Depression can lead to addiction; the strain and stresses of life, to abuse. Resist the temptation to 'transmit'; be compassionate and understanding and don't believe the nonsense people tell you. Or, sometimes, that *you* tell you. Make allowance for the chaos of individual lives.

Rescue a starfish. Make a difference to just one person. It's unlikely to be as easy as chucking a starfish back into the sea, but stick with it and you will find your own life is better for it.

Resolve to offer practical support. Those who are dealing with the most vulnerable and marginalised groups in our society need help, so help them in any way you can. From hands-on help at your local school, to pressurising your local councillors or sorting food at the local food bank.

7

Generosity at Home

'That best portion of a good man's life, his little,
unremembered acts of kindness and of love.'

William Wordsworth, poet

Help others, help ourselves, listen ...

Given the choice between an inward-looking, acquisitive, worried existence centred on self, and a generous, open and engaged life centred on others, the decision should be easy. A generous life is a happier life and it's good to make it a habit. And Act 1, Scene 1 of a more generous life is simply to start being more generous towards those closest to us: our family, friends, work colleagues, and move outwards to those who might not be expecting it; people on the outer edge of our social radar. And by generous I mean not just financially, but empathetically too.

Everyone has it within them to become a significant and powerful force for good, no matter what life has thrown at them. Some people are natural listeners and have great empathy; they're the sort of people who are always there for us when we need them. The rest of us can be like them if we just pause for breath and think. And when we start to focus on others, we find a sense of purpose that gives us a sense of proportion and balance against all our own struggles and difficulties.

In relationships, everyone is different. To get through difficult times (in marriage, with your kids, at work, parenting teenagers, being a teenager, supporting people who are just downright difficult or who don't share your view of life) you need to understand that difference and listen to whoever is talking to you, reflect back to them that you have understood (which means not butting in with your views but keeping quiet at this point) and only when you really understand, help them come up with *their* solutions – not yours. All this requires you to give time and headspace to people.

Volunteers at the Samaritans are trained not to give advice, but to listen. When the Reverend Chad Varah originally founded the charity in 1953, his plan was to give people who were lonely and suicidal the benefit of his professional counselling. So many people queued to see him that he got a whole load of volunteers to make cups of tea and chat until those queuing could be ushered into his presence. And, much to his surprise, cups of tea and someone to chat to meant that most people received the help they needed without seeing him at all. Over sixty years later, the Samaritans have 108 paid staff and 21,200 volunteers.

What is the purpose of life? In part it is to be there for other people who need you. Sometimes that, in itself, is enough to give purpose to a day.

Put yourself in someone else's shoes rather than banging on about your life, your worries and your triumphs and disasters. Make time for others; listen before you speak or suggest a solution; remember that your perspective may not be relevant to the person you're speaking to. It's their life: empathise. Focus on the person you're talking to, resist the temptation to broadcast. Whilst they're talking, keep quiet. Don't interrupt.

You won't become a saint overnight, or get a mention in the New Year's Honours list (not yet anyway!), but in deciding to help others you will change and enhance your own life as much as theirs, for many years ahead. Isn't that an amazing thought?

... and act

'What we think, or what we know, or what we believe is in the end of little consequence; the only consequence is what we do.'

John Ruskin, social thinker and philanthropist

It is deeply rewarding to engage our gentle and caring side in helping others. To show love, kindness, thoughtfulness and empathy. To show our best part, the *real* us, which can get buried underneath the hustle, stress and problems of everyday life. That's the part that is moved by music, cries during soppy films, loves good friends and is actually touched by the plight of others in this country and around the world. As the Dalai Lama said: 'If you want others to be happy, practise compassion. If you want to be happy, practise compassion. '

How is everybody?

Where has eye contact gone? On the street, in pubs and even restaurants, it's eyes down for your mobile/iPad. On the train, laptop open, work or watch a film. Mobile on, text, play games. Send an email to a colleague sitting at the next desk rather than get up and speak to them. All the while muttering about email overload! We text people not in the room rather than talk to those who are. With space at a premium, many new-build homes don't allow for a table to sit round for a family meal (despite research showing this is important). Many families are separated by miles or by continents. We take a new job, we walk away. We take the job filled with weeks of international travel and find our friends are too busy to see us when we get back. We take the contract for a few years on the other side of the world and when we move on we need to start over again.

It's all too easy to lose touch – we know so many people and yet really know so few. In just a few months jobs can be lost, careers surge or a terminal illness can strike. Teens often speak a different language from their parents and almost inevitably from their grandparents. 'I find it depressing,' muttered a contact assessing juvenile mental health in the UK, 'that charities seem to be picking up a whole load of stuff that families and friends would have done a generation or so ago. And they can never replace what a family could have given in love and care.' Quite.

Generosity should start with your family, friends and work colleagues, and extend to people you vaguely know, or know by sight only, whom you might otherwise pass with a nod or a fleeting smile. Your actions and behaviour influence everyone you're in contact with on a regular basis. There is always a ripple effect. People close to you need your help, so before you start 'saving the world', pause and think of those closest to you: start practising in-reach before you try outreach.

Why don't you set some time aside from your busy, stressful, fascinating or boring life to think about other people and their lives? Put a decent amount of time in your diary within the next seven days. Try to make sure that you don't have to be somewhere or doing something for a couple of hours. Because this is just the beginning of what will turn out to be a really interesting, involving and positive experience.

Choose a quiet spot where you won't be interrupted, where you can turn off your mobile and where no one will disturb you: a room at home; a favourite spot in the garden; a rug under a tree or beside a river; a bench looking out to sea; a local church. Have with you a pad of paper, a pen and your address book or contacts list to prompt ideas (OK, maybe you have to turn your mobile back on for this!). Settle down with just yourself and your thoughts.

Your mission is to think about the people you know from *their* perspective. Try to imagine yourself in their shoes. This can be quite difficult, especially trying to override your pre-conceptions and judgements of other people, their behaviour and mannerisms. *How is everybody?* It is quite extraordinary how focusing your mind on another person's life for five minutes will give you a new insight into their world and some of the situations they are facing. We are all so busy and so concerned about our own lives, our own triumphs and concerns, that the problems of even our closest friends often pass us by completely.

Are they happy? Pretty content and on good form? Is it their birthday soon (and are you about to forget it?) or are they about to celebrate something? Are they going for a job interview or have they just started a new job; taken an important exam or just passed one; moved home or retired? Are they well? Is it time to congratulate them on something or wish them good luck? Are you totally out of touch? Ring, email or write a quick note. Now!

It usually takes a quiet moment or more to get through the bravado. For people to open up and admit they are finding life a bit tough. They need to believe you genuinely care. Perhaps they are unhappy, stressed or ill; facing serious challenges at work or having problems with a relationship. Are they lonely or struggling with money worries? What sort of problems are they facing?

One in five people get seriously depressed at some stage. So if you have more than five people on your list, odds are someone will be feeling more than temporarily down. I suffered a bout of severe clinical depression in my mid-forties and fortunately, with some excellent medical help, exercise, prayer and wonderful support from those closest to me, I made a complete recovery. At my lowest ebb, when I had become deeply vulnerable and incapable of sensible thought or behaviour, the generosity of family and friends was immeasurable and very loving. By being quite open about it I suddenly found numerous 'normal' friends who were fellow sufferers, most of whom had never dared to tell anyone who didn't need to know.

Everyone has their own problems and we are all insecure, however confident we may seem. Your mission is to think about those closest to you and the challenges they face and then do something that tells them you care. Generosity of thought followed by generosity of action.

Make time for this now or you will put it off. Remember, it is the little things you do that really help and procrastination doesn't help at all. No one is aware they are in your thoughts unless you touch base and tell them.

Generosity to family

'Oh, do we *have* to?' you groan. Challenging, this one, isn't it? Think about your ageing parents, your in-laws, the sister who's moved away (with her very dull husband), your brother (with whom you have nothing in common), your cousin (with whom you fell out when he/she behaved impossibly at a family wedding). You may think it is just your family, but in my experience everyone has some no-go areas with their nearest and dearest.

In an ideal world, our relationships with those closest to us would be the warmest and most loving. But whilst there's a shared family history, it doesn't follow that family members are all alike, or even compatible. You don't have to be a psychologist to realise that those we know best we often judge most harshly. After all, we know all about their questionable habits, weaknesses and sometimes nasty little ways. As they do ours. We can hold grudges for years, and family dynamics can endure for decades. The younger sibling is always expected to play second fiddle to the elder, even when they're approaching retirement themselves. Old habits die hard.

And, of course, the really depressing fact is that if you have a problem or a dispute with a member of your family – whatever the cause, whoever did what to whom and whoever was right or wrong – it is hard to forgive. We have all heard: 'I will never speak to him/her again.' My father wasn't really on speaking terms with his brother; my father-in-law had a similar situation with his brother. I don't think either set had a lot in common, but it did seem an awful waste.

Many years back, my wife and I went on a marriage course. We didn't go because our marriage was on the rocks, we went because it sounded interesting. The course reaffirmed all those things a couple knows they're meant to do but that are all too easy to forget. Give each other one-to-one time; listen to each other; forgive. The same applies to any long-term relationship. 'Love is an active verb' we were reminded. 'You need to make an effort.'

Generosity to friends

'From quiet homes and first beginning, out to the undiscovered ends, there's nothing worth the wear of winning, but laughter and the love of friends.'

Hilaire Belloc, writer and historian

How are your friends? The really good friends you haven't seen for ages, but would love to catch up with again. The people whom you know well and those you would like to get to know better. Where are they? When did you last see them? Are they OK or do they need a hug?

Keeping in touch via Facebook isn't really keeping in touch. A new phrase entering our vocabulary is 'computer alienation'. People most often don't post about the issues they're dealing with. So wasting time with a friend is not wasting time. Swapping news and just being together for no particular purpose is a true blessing and part of what friendships are all about. Put time aside to make sure you catch up. Prioritise this over an extra hour at the office. Nurture great, long-lasting friendships at least as much as time spent socialising with new and potentially interesting acquaintances.

You could try your hand at Desert Island Friends. In Radio 4's *Desert Island Discs*, guests are cast away on a desert island with the Bible, the complete works of Shakespeare, a luxury and eight favourite pieces of music. In Desert Island Friends, instead of your eight favourite pieces of music, you can take eight friends with you, including family members. It can be a very sobering thought. Most people can't actually think of eight and many wouldn't take members of their own family.

Generosity at work

You spend a great deal of time with your work colleagues. Some are a laugh; others seem really friendly but you don't see much of them during the day; some you wouldn't trust further than you can throw them; others are hugely ambitious and don't have a life; some have been there for most of their adult lives and live for the weekends or to pursue an eccentric hobby! Without doubt, many will also be stressed about their kids, the health of someone dear to them or what to do about their ageing parents.

Grab an internal contact list. Go through it and think for a moment about your colleagues' lives and what you know of them. Perhaps go to lunch with someone you usually wouldn't or have a drink with them after work. You will be pleasantly surprised by how often people's lives and interests outside work will make them more approachable and reveal them as fellow humans! And you as a better colleague.

Management team-building games can provide a common framework where surprising one-to-one conversations happen. My cousin told me of a management programme where the methodology was to take people out of their comfort zone, facilitating communication and understanding between colleagues at a much more profound level. A close colleague of his talked about the fact that she had a very traumatic upbringing, including being abused. He was extremely moved, and his point to me was that he would never have known this without 'getting out of the office'.

'It is amazing what you can accomplish if you do not care who gets the credit'

Harry S. Truman, US President 1945–1953

When people confide to me that 'my job's become a nightmare' and I ask why, the answer is almost invariably because of a difficult boss or colleague: a working relationship that has broken down. It's about bullying or blocking or someone else taking the credit for work done or just being 'totally impossible to work with'. And, of course, the reverse is true. 'The team I work with is awesome (fantastic/inspiring/great fun).'

It's not rocket science to work out which team will achieve more: the happy one or the one tearing itself apart. Getting your mojo going when you're feeling miserable is hard. So let's try to be as generous and nurturing at work as we can, whomever we work for. Encourage mentoring, buddy schemes and time out where you can really listen. Make yourself as approachable as possible. Lighten someone else's load when you can. Care about the people you spend your working hours with. Enjoy the ripple effect.

THE MILLWRIGHT WHO DIED:
A STORY FROM *LEADERSHIP IS AN ART*

Max De Pree was CEO of Herman Miller in the 1980s; a company founded by his father. He purposefully set about creating an inclusive and caring company where everyone had a say and he championed 'erring on the side of over-communication'. His book, *Leadership Is an Art*, was first published in 1987 and is still available. What follows is an extract.

In the furniture industry of the 1920s, the machines of most facto-ries were not run by electric motors, but by pulleys from a central drive shaft which was run by steam.

The steam engine got its steam from the boiler. The boiler got its fuel from the sawdust and other waste coming out of the machine room – a beautiful cycle.

The millwright was the person who oversaw that cycle and on whom the entire activity of the operation depended. He was the key person.

One night the millwright died.

My father, a young manager at the time, did not particularly know what he should do, but he thought he should go and visit the family. He went to the house and was invited to join the family in the living room. There was some awkward conversation – the kind with which many of us are familiar.

The widow asked my father if it would be all right if she read aloud some poetry. Naturally he agreed. She went into another room, came back with a bound book, and for many minutes read selected pieces of beautiful poetry. When she was finished, my father commented on how beautiful the poetry was and asked who wrote it. She replied that her husband, the millwright, was the poet.

> *It is now nearly sixty years since the millwright died and my*
> *father and many of us at Herman Miller continue to wonder: was*
> *he a poet who did a millwright's work, or was he a millwright who*
> *wrote poetry?*

Just as there was more to the millwright than his job, there is more
to most people than we first see, or choose to see, often because
we don't actually care or bother to find out. We make assumptions based on our personal perspectives. We ask 'What do you
do?' not 'Tell me about you. Who are you?' We judge people by
their dress and – often temporary – status, rather than valuing
their experience and wisdom. We fail to see them in the round.

Generosity towards people you hardly know

We tend to be drawn to people who are similar to ourselves,
or whom we admire, and spend most of our time with them.
There is nothing wrong with this, but for a moment I would like
you to think of the people on the edges of your radar, whom
you wouldn't normally socialise with or even think of talking
to. You might find them boring – people who are quite simply
someone else's problem. (As the saying has it, one definition of a
drinks party is 'a gathering where everyone present is a crashing
bore – except you'!)

My mother-in-law, Eleanor, always insisted that no one was
boring if you asked them about themselves and then listened to
them. 'Rubbish,' I would tell her. 'Some people are as dull as
ditchwater.' But I learnt that she was completely right and no
one is boring if you persevere. People's most interesting subject
is themselves. Ask them about their family (good one for parents
who are generally besotted by their children) or their work

(some people do very dull jobs, or jobs that an average person finds totally incomprehensible, but at least by asking them about it you learn about that area of life).

I always ask people: 'What do you do when you are not being dynamic?' Followed by: 'Are you a lethal tennis player, a frustrated opera singer, an obsessed fisherman?' Touch on a person's interest and you will have their attention for ages. You are likely to learn something new, even interesting, and may find yourself going through entire parties without anyone asking you anything about your own life. And that's OK.

There's always someone who needs someone. Many times, they are the person who is generally shunned, politely ignored or actively avoided by yourself and others. These people have a very hard life and often a terribly lonely time too. They are people who need a kind word or act to lift their spirits. Yet we label them 'problem people', dull or difficult, or simply write them off as no-hopers. The people who face discrimination because they're disabled, have lost the plot mentally, look different or are easy to make fun of.

Everyone has heard of the biblical parable of the Good Samaritan. Jesus tells a lawyer that he should love his neighbour as much as he loves himself. 'Who is my neighbour?' replies the man (they can be quite pedantic, these lawyers).

Let's remind ourselves of the parable ...

A man was travelling from Jerusalem to Jericho when he was attacked by robbers who stripped and beat him and left him half dead. The next person to arrive was a priest who saw the man lying on the road and passed by on the other side. Then came a Levite. He did exactly the same. The third passer-by was a Samaritan. When he saw the man, he was moved with compassion, came to him and treated and bound up his wounds. Then he put him on his own animal and brought him to an inn so that he could take care of him properly. When the Samaritan had to leave the next day, he gave the innkeeper two days' money to look after the injured man's needs with instructions to carry on doing whatever was necessary to look after him with assurances that if more money was needed, the Samaritan would pay the difference on his return journey.

Having told the parable, Jesus asked the lawyer which of the three had been a good neighbour.

'He who showed mercy.'

'Then go and do likewise.'

One of the key points of the parable is the different motivations. The priest and the Levite were religious leaders (Levites helped priests in the temples) yet they put their self-interest first. (Touching the poor man risked making them unclean so they left him to die.) The Samaritan was one of society's outcasts and wouldn't have come from that neighbourhood; so was not a 'neighbour' by any definition. Yet he stopped and helped. He did everything he could and more. The Samaritan would have been looked upon as the lowest of the low in biblical times, but *he* acted. Those who should and could have helped, didn't.

The unmentioned question the priest and the Levite asked themselves was: 'If I stop to help this man, what will happen to me?' The Samaritan reversed the question and asked: 'If I do not stop to help this man, what will happen to him?' The parable is so well-known that academics all over the world examine 'The Samaritan Paradox'. Is the motivation to help in part because we expect reciprocity? And therefore it's selfish after all? But the Samaritan of the parable was not from the area and was already outcast. He was helping a stranger who, intriguingly, is the only person in the story not identified. Reciprocity doesn't seem to be part of his story. It is about a man who obviously needed help but wasn't capable of asking for it.

Now own up. How many times have you deliberately 'passed by on the other side'? There's a YouTube clip where someone is filmed tripping over on a city pavement: a man falls over hard and struggles to get up. The same man acts two parts. When dressed in a suit, people stop to help him. Dressed as if he could be homeless, they look, then pass him by, not offering to help, even though it's full daylight and there are plenty of people around to guarantee safety.

Have you ever ignored someone's plea for help, or known someone who was having a difficult time but avoided asking them about it for fear of 'getting too involved'? Have you avoided someone because you see 'homeless', 'alcoholic', 'waster' – not the person? You might have hurried on with your own life, because you were slightly scared and anyway you are very busy, and someone else will step in. But homeless people are people: they appreciate a chat as much as a cup of coffee. By 'seeing' them as individuals you transmit empathy, kindness and hope.

Develop your Generous Gene

It really is the little, unexpected acts of generosity that people remember and are touched by. They take thought and a bit of effort, but invariably cost very little. Little things matter a lot.

Put some time aside in your diary. Think about individual members of your family. How are they? Ring a couple of them that you haven't spoken to recently and ask them. How are your friends? The people you really love, admire, trust, laugh with, have known since you were at school. Arrange a catch-up – even if they live in another part of the country or another country altogether. Call. Email.

Think about work. Who do you not know much about at work, but have often been curious about? Or felt sorry for? One of my friends was prompted by this idea to ask his secretary out for lunch – she was very surprised but they had fun and learned more about how each other ticked. Result? A better working relationship.

Cheer someone up. Who do you know who is having a difficult time? Make space to talk to them, ask them how they are and encourage them. Most of all, listen. Remember the saying: 'God gave us two eyes, two ears and one mouth.' Use them in that order!

Visit the hospital. Some patients get no visitors. Ring your local hospital, ask for their visitors' group and ask them who needs cheering up.

Be a Good Samaritan. Go out of your way to help someone you don't know at all. This week. Quietly. Do any of the people on the margins of your life need help? What could you do today, in the next few days, or when you might next connect, that would help them in a practical way and show them that you care about them? Treat the next homeless person you pass in the street as a person first. Stop and have a chat.

Be secretly and surprisingly generous. Become someone who 'pays it forward': buy a book token and place it in a bestseller so the next person who picks it up can have it for free; hand a fiver to the flower seller and ask them to give flowers to someone who would appreciate them; secretly treat the people in the queue behind you to their cappuccinos (and start taking your coffee at 'Suspended Coffee' outlets); do the same for a cinema ticket; pay the car toll for the car behind you as well; let someone keep the change.

Spread the work of The Kindness Offensive by joining in. It's about having fun and sharing – distributing free tickets, food, chocolates, kitchen equipment etc. to people who need it, via charities and directly. Not a charity, not a business, 'just a group of people with a phone having fun giving stuff away'. In just over six years they have fed over 2 million people and given away over £5 million worth of stuff, including Christmas presents to every single child in London hospitals and 100,000 books. Have fun with it! There's no excuse not to. www.thekindnessoffensive.com

Practise Random Acts of Kindness. Be inspired when you check out the website. They've a suggestion for every day: hold a door open for someone with a buggy; help a kid with their homework; let another driver go first; pick up some litter; pay a compliment to the person at the supermarket check-out. Or just smile and be nice to people! Ideas easy to find through www.randomactsofkindness.org and also www.40acts.org.uk.

Join the organ donor register. If everyone in the UK did, there would be enough healthy organs for everyone, saving three lives a day, as well as big savings on the NHS advertising budget. www.organdonation.nhs.uk

Sign up to give blood. As they say on the website, 96 per cent of us rely on the 4 per cent who do. www.blood.co.uk

8

Generous Communities

Your country needs YOU!

We don't live in a fair and equal society where, to quote St Benedict in the sixth century, 'the rich have an aim and the vulnerable somewhere to turn to'. Whether we swing left or right politically, it seems impossible there will ever be enough tax revenue to pay for the welfare support we think we deserve. So if we want to create a better, fairer and more compassionate country we have to roll up our sleeves and get stuck in.

We have the solution and it lies within every one of us. We just need to help out. We can move society on by proactively caring about the community of people we know and the people we connect with; by taking steps to develop our Generous Gene. How great to feel part of the movement changing our culture from a focus on having to a focus on happiness and quality of life. From social breakdown to something more hopeful – a caring economy.

When he was chief rabbi, Jonathan Sacks wrote *The Politics of Hope*: a wonderfully lucid argument for social cohesion as the way to create a more peaceful, prosperous society – a society held together by voluntary 'covenants' rather than legally based 'contracts'. When I read it some paragraphs simply leapt off the page! Here's one, about Alexis de Tocqueville (1805–1859):

> *Tocqueville was haunted by one fear. A liberal, democratic, capitalist society would eventually lose its own liberty. Not by revolution, but through a slow erosion of the ties that bind people to one another. It would evolve ... because of the retreat of individuals into the private sphere and the growth of the state ... gradually and without resistance. Tocqueville searched for a phrase to describe this, to him, quite novel danger. At times he called it 'administrative despotism'.*
>
> *What might protect a nation against such a fate? Tocqueville had no doubt. It was the strength of 'associations'. The only way a sense of fellowship can be regained is by voluntary associations, and it was this that formed the defence of liberty in a democratic society.*

'Administrative despotism'! That touches a chord. Having done recent battle with various local government departments to get some care for an elderly and extremely vulnerable friend living over a hundred miles away, it seems pretty clear to me that administrative procedures definitely get in the way of action. A century and a half after Tocqueville, administrative despotism is alive and thriving! And that's even before we get to stretched budgets and over-stretched (and often low-paid) staff juggling impossible workloads.

So if this isn't the world we want for our elderly friends (or anyone else dependent on similar resources), let's do something about it.

A better world

At first sight, all this seems like a cause for despair, a cast-iron case for leaving the country, emigrating to ... I'm really not sure where anymore. For countless groups of us, the subject matter for hours of gloomy conversation is about Britain's final demise: 'Will the last person to leave these islands please turn off the lights?'

We now need to be gently radical to have any hope of addressing the *cause*, not just the symptoms. There is a better world out there. The optimist in me says we can regain a bit of spirit in adversity and show that we care about the people with whom we share these small islands. Communities are at the heart of real and lasting change because they can address every aspect of their local environment. Great change happens when we start involving ourselves in the warp and weft of community life; not accepting the status quo, but taking matters into our own hands. I may not be able to be physically present for my elderly friend, but I can at least call regularly and step up to the challenge for someone who lives nearer me.

So let's actively engage in generosity and start by helping our own communities; undertaking and carrying out *ourselves* the numerous small but important tasks that don't meet the ever-shrinking criteria of our hard-pressed social services, NHS, education system, *et al.* Just do it!

Regenerating community

The good news is that our villages, towns and cities are just that, ours, to become involved in, to change and to improve. They are full of grass-roots and imaginative community groups all working quietly to make life better. There is a paradigm shift already happening. From Kinsale in Ireland via Totnes in Devon, the Transition Town movement has become a global phenomenon in under a decade.

The core idea is to encourage the connections that get people thinking about how they can create great, resilient, abundant communities; communities more independent and in control of their own futures. There's no 'one size fits all'. People get together and work out what they want to focus on. Support for local businesses can come in the form of local currencies to be used only when you buy local goods or services. National and global chains aren't allowed to join this scheme, which is a pretty powerful way of keeping local money local, rather than siphoned off to fund plans of global domination somewhere else. And, of course, keeping local money flowing has a multiplier effect.

Local Entrepreneur Forums are a relatively recent development: 'Everyone has a stake and everyone has something to offer ... it isn't all about the money.' The forums are a friendly Dragon's Den, where people pledge anything from money to help with childcare. They have quickly moved from Totnes, where the idea first started, to take root in Brixton and Gothenburg, Sweden, too. 'Don't wait' is the message, 'Just rise up and do it'. Helping each other is contagious, exciting and fun.

Tackling issues

Of course, part of the UK's DNA is its strong, well-established charitable sector – over 195,000 registered charities at the last count raising and spending £80 billion every year. They are increasingly supplemented by newer, expanding social enterprises – organisations where under 50 per cent of the profit finds its way to enrich shareholders and where the motivation is much more about doing good. The latest estimates are around 68,000 organisations claiming to operate as social enterprises and the sector just keeps growing. As do community interest companies (CICs). 10,000 organisations putting community benefit before profit.

Charities aren't immune from huge pressures on budgets. The irony is that now, when cuts in public funding are hitting a whole range of services, there are more needy people out there than ever. The perfect storm. The largest funder of the UK charity sector in the recent past has been the government. Governments of different persuasions ask charities to pitch for business as a matter of routine; increasingly against private-sector companies, whose ethos allows them to cherry-pick or to fund a loss-making contract to enter a potentially lucrative area of work.

At their best, charities are innovators and entrepreneurs. They are often established because someone has become incensed by something that's just not fair and is determined to do something about it. They carry on because they are determined to overcome the odds and find better solutions. They do a huge amount to inform government policy, as well as getting on with the job of looking after some of the most marginalised groups in society: children on whom everyone else has given up, offenders, victims of domestic violence. Research into brain injuries, Alzheimer's, Parkinson's, multiple sclerosis and many more life-threatening conditions would be nowhere near as advanced without the efforts of and funding from charities. They connect us with a cause, handle the bureaucracy where it (inevitably) exists, lobby hard to obtain central and regional government funding and fight with their supporters on everyone's behalf for a more even playing field.

Where would our countryside and heritage be without the National Trust, RSPB or even thousands of village fêtes in aid of the local church restoration fund? Where would our culture be without public-supported institutions like the Tate, the Natural History Museum and the Edinburgh Festival? To say nothing of our ability and willingness to support overseas crises through the Disasters Emergency Committee, UNICEF, Oxfam, the Red Cross and more.

There is a charity for every cause, sometimes several competing charities, caring for every possible social and physical need. If you are not already formally or informally linked to one or more, now is the time to do something about it.

A COINCIDENCE? DOUG'S STORY

I met Doug for the first time after being e-introduced by a friend. We swapped 'news headlines' at a coffee shop in Euston station – he told me about his very successful tech businesses and I told him about my work with charities and philanthropy. He was about to start a tech hub in a particular city in the north of England.

'I know it,' I replied, 'I was there just a couple of months ago, visiting a wonderful small charity supporting extremely vulnerable and disadvantaged young people. It's a desert of social deprivation.'

Doug asked me exactly where the charity operated and I told him.

'I was born there,' he grinned. 'And in fact, until recently, my parents still lived there.'

So it was a natural next step to introduce him to the leader of the charity. They met twice and since then Doug, some of his team and his family have been actively helping the charity and supporting the young people with job training and other opportunities. And they have introduced others.

Both of us are even now slightly amazed by the serendipity of the short 'blind date' coffee and its outcomes. If there is a lesson here it is that two people focused on actually 'doing' something to help others can find it extraordinarily easy to do so.

Volunteering

You might be surprised at the number of people you know who spend a little time each week doing something useful to help others, even when they already have a demanding day job. Often, they do it quietly, on a regular basis, without making a fuss. You could do it too.

Researchers have been crawling over our motivations again and they have found that people who volunteer are happier with their work-life balance – which means happier per se. So there is something in it for everyone.

And that's what millions of us have been finding out. Did you know, 19.8 million of us claim to be actively involved in volunteering in our own communities every year? Many of your friends and work colleagues will already be involved in fund-raising, helping out as a carer or mentor, acting as a trustee or school governor or just pitching in wherever is needed. And, on the other hand, and just as likely, someone you know will be being looked after or supported by a charity, even though they may never tell you.

There are over a million charity trustees for a start. University Freshers' Week stalls include a whole section on volunteering for students who want to get involved. Pressed for time? Check out micro-volunteering and online volunteering; low-key, informal, bite-size volunteering that fits around the rest of your life. Bake a cake, complete a questionnaire, serve at a stall for an hour. Thirty minutes a week adds up to over two days across a year. Match your interests with a local cause through www.do-it.org, a national charity that can link you to suitable local opportunities.

THE FOOD CHAIN

A friend shared this story: 'Once, when our three children were very, very young (three under the age of three), a friend rang in the middle of the afternoon and said, 'Don't cook supper. I'm bringing some round at five.' We waited with great anticipation. Sure enough, on the pip of five, she appeared with a chicken casserole, potatoes and salad. Supper was handed over on the doorstep. This gift really touched us and has inspired me to do the same. A cake or supper – unsolicited – makes people's hearts soft. It's simple, unexpected and it works. Surprise is definitely a key element!'

So don't wait to be asked. People don't like to be seen as needy. And of course they'll manage without you, but that's not the point.

My local neighbourhood now operates a well-established Food Chain. People agree to cook and deliver meals as part of an informal rota. All it takes is somebody willing to co-ordinate and once someone is on the radar a quick email gets offers coming in. Those in need could be convalescing from an operation, in the middle of chemotherapy, looking after a sick child or a new baby, suffering a bereavement – whatever it is that's making life difficult. The Food Chain is alerted and people put their hands up to cook and deliver a meal, sometimes regular meals over a few weeks. The group is big enough now to provide a continuous stream of 'real' ready meals, almost all out-of-the-oven fresh.

Many of those helped initially insist they are fine, but in truth they are always touched by the kindness, bowled over by the idea that someone they might not even know has taken the time to do this for them, and cheered by contact with someone who has set aside some time to brighten up their day. The impact is much greater than just a meal you haven't had to think about.

And you won't be surprised to learn that the people cooking and delivering all this food enjoy doing it (cooking an extra portion or two is, after all, very little extra effort). A casual neighbourly conversation which before may have been 'Did you know?' translates quickly into 'I can help'.

As impressive and heart-warming as all this is, what really hits home is the incredible simplicity of the Food Chain. There are enough cooks involved not to over-burden anyone and it all just 'happens' with the minimum of fuss and drama.

Less talk, more action

All it takes is action. There's no need to be formal about it, though there could be an opportunity to link into a charity that already exists. We often think about doing a bit more locally, knowing that it is good to help other people and good to do something worthwhile with our lives. We *talk* about it a great deal, but somehow never get round to it. 'One day, when I have more time ...' we say. But the time to start giving and being useful is *now*, not tomorrow. If we want to make our country a more civilised place to live, now and for future generations, we have to create the greatest change by doing it ourselves. Take the kids along with you if you can. *We* are the amorphous 'grass-roots' and 'hard-to-reach groups' who know what's going on and can do something about it. We don't need layers of bureaucracy to find out or to get started. By getting out there we will build connections, trust and a true sense of a community that's a great place to live.

It is time to grab the chance before people die of loneliness and lack of care because we are too busy. The plain truth is that we have absolutely no guarantee of a tomorrow. For my elderly friend, now unable to get out and about, a short chat with a neighbour or friend lifts her spirits much more than a short chat with her carer. And, knowing her, I'm willing to bet she's not alerted several acquaintances who might be more than happy to visit, because she's being stoic and 'doesn't want to be a bother', even though that attitude goes with being depressed. So don't wait to be asked for help, because sometimes that request never comes – do it on your own initiative. Do it today.

The opportunity to help out might vanish completely while we are 'thinking about it' or 'waiting for more time' or not calling someone 'because they haven't called me'. Peter Melchett, a former director of Greenpeace, has said: 'I prefer the optimism of action to the pessimism of thought.'

'THE POWER OF SMALL ACTIONS IS AWESOME': PAM'S STORY

This story starts with three people sitting round their kitchen table thinking about how they might bring their small market town in the north of England together. How they could find a unifying language that would cut across everyone – irrespective of age, income or culture. The answer they came up with was food. And what started as a seed swap became a herb garden; became taking unused, wasteland round the town and turning it into vegetable beds for the community to tend and pick and share; became the Incredible Edible Todmorden way of doing things – and, to quote Pam Warhurst, one of its founders, 'We've done it all without a flipping strategy document.'

They asked themselves: 'What could we do to create a revolution about the way we interact with each other?' and 'How

173

could people invest in more kindness to each other and the environment?' Everyone is part of the jigsaw. Everyone is part of the solution. They have a motto: 'If you eat, you're in.' No one is left out. Help yourself to the food you see growing – it's free.

The artists in the community design labelling for the beds so anyone who has never seen fruit and veg actually growing knows what to pick when; a plot at an old people's home enables the residents to plant, grow and eat the produce; people who like cooking run demonstrations. There is now a tourist green route through the town past the plots of 'incredible edibles' and via many of the local, independent retailers and the market. Trade is up. In just three and a half years local schools have become involved, the high school has started to teach agriculture and there's a new market garden training centre on donated land. There's much, much more; it's a joined-up idea with growing food linked to learning and to business. The Todmorden experiment has now been replicated in 30 towns in the UK and from Japan to Latin America, USA to New Zealand. 'And it's just volunteers and it's only an experiment.' And it started with no budget.

As Pam Warhurst says, 'Through an organic process we are starting to believe in ourselves again. I have seen the power of small actions and it is awesome.'

What the community started is working so well that their local authority has decided to create an asset register of spare land for food banks for communities to use, and also asked their staff to help the communities grow and maintain their spaces. This is public spiritedness that not only builds a stronger local community, but has gained the traction to involve and influence local government. It's an example of true integration started by people who decided for themselves that they could and should create a better life.

A not so quiet revolution

Thanks to social media, there is already more bottom-up engagement. More of us questioning, signing petitions and contacting our MPs about the things we care about. We can whip up a storm in weeks or even days. We can lobby on issues that didn't get a pre-election airing. Whilst still in a minority, we increasingly feel we can make ourselves heard: 41 per cent of us feel we have a say in what government does – against less than a third back in the 1980s.

---

38 DEGREES

The UK campaigning organisation 38 Degrees was in its infancy at the time of the 2010 election. In five years, it's grown to 3 million members and has been called 'the real opposition' by the *New Statesman*. They regularly poll their members asking them to prioritise what's most important, to identify the issues they really care about. 38 Degrees may simplify the debate, they may even sometimes get it wrong, but it's information and a call to action at a time when the outcome can be influenced – 'Write to your MP this week as there is a vote this Thursday.' They create online videos watched by millions, as well as social media campaigns with similar numbers of people signing up. Before the 2015 election they uncovered the 'Mayfair Tax Loophole' – a totally legal tax-avoidance mechanism used by the wealthiest – and encouraged journalists to make it a campaign issue.

What really grabs my attention is that 38 Degrees has evolved from its original focus on online lobbying to more direct and local action. It is both localism in action and national in influence, being asked to represent the views of its members to parliamentary committees. Taking an instant poll, the 38 Degrees community can contribute their views in the days leading up to any major parliamentary meeting, informed by the agenda. Groups of members engage their MPs face-to-face in their own constituency, man stalls in shopping centres and on high streets getting support for petitions, and take to the phones to spread awareness. From an online, numbers-based model, members are now connecting in small groups at coffee shops across the country. What was bottom-up involvement at a national level is increasingly operating very locally as well. And it's entirely funded by lots of people chipping in small amounts of their own cash to support a better democracy.

You and I now have the information at our fingertips to get involved both nationally and locally. Sign up to 38 Degrees and you will be alerted ahead of critical parliamentary votes, so you can decide if you want to lobby your MP. My local Neighbourhood Watch sends out regular emails. I am alerted to scams, and the Community Officer thanks everyone for drawing attention to criminal activity and making my neighbourhood safer. If I notice an unsafe paving stone or fly tipping I just tap in my postcode and report it on www.FixMyStreet.com.

It seems the concept of a post-bureaucratic age is already in motion and with it the reality of more of us acting locally 'without a flipping strategy document' and using our lobbying power for the issues we really care about. And the experience is often that our actions generate more immediate and more effective change than the current public services. They can only become more responsive as we increasingly communicate directly with our local politicians and councils, hospitals and utility companies about improvements to services, or simply experiment by doing some of them ourselves. The possibilities are limitless, but there's certainly hope here of public services working in tandem with, and encouraging, community-interest groups for better, quicker results. We can all play a part in creating more peaceful, thriving local communities.

Develop your Generous Gene

Here is a starter 'put your hand up' list. You can no doubt add many more. You absolutely don't need to wait till you retire.

Volunteer. Is there an issue on your doorstep that makes you cross? Litter? Kids roaming the streets? Disability? Old age? The state of the local park? Search out local charities and offer your help. There are more small grass-roots organisations beavering away than you could possibly imagine, as well as a whole load of national organisations operating locally. Get in touch with Do-it (www.do-it.org), Volunteering England (www.volunteering.org. uk), or Reach and Pilot Light if you want to use your business experience and professional skills (www.reachskills.org.uk and www.pilotlight.org.uk).

Be brave and start something. Follow the example of our Todmorden friends or start a Food Chain. Be bold. Many, many initiatives begin with a gathering round the kitchen table to change the local landscape – sometimes literally. Clear a pond, plant some herbs, involve the kids, put some flyers up and see where this leads you. Experiment. Action is the only thing that ever changed anything.

Link up. Join your local Transition Town group or one of the growing number of informal networks bringing businesses, sole traders and non-profits together to work out how to share expertise and create local win-wins. Change soulless suburbs into places where people take a real interest in each other's welfare and business successes. If your town's not a Transition Town, should it be? Or is the urban model of something like Kentish Clusters (www.kentishcluster.com) more appropriate?

Sign up to 38 Degrees. The online campaign group that encourages you to lobby for change at critical moments when 'our values are at stake and we can make a difference'. More and more members are meeting up to act locally and offline, collecting signatures, delivering petitions to MPs or meeting them, but this is 100 per cent optional. www.38degrees.org.uk

Help the school. If you enjoy being around children, simply offer your services to your community's schools. Expect to be security (DBS) checked. You might end up mentoring, providing homework support and/or reading help or helping teachers supervise outings or breaks.

Be a taxi. With a bit of free time you could help ferry elderly or disabled people around. Look up 'Community Transport'. There might be a local community bus service, but a private car is more flexible and you can also have a decent conversation with someone who is housebound and a bit starved of company. A friend of mine once volunteered to take a boy who had been hurt playing hockey to hospital. She took him there, waited for him to be treated then took him back to school. She has continued to do school 'medical runs' for several years.

Take someone shopping. I know you can do it online or pick up someone's shopping list, but that's not the point. Many elderly people don't have a computer, or their eyesight makes using one difficult. They appreciate contact, being able to get out, see what's available and maybe do a little impulse shopping. It's also a bonus to be with someone who can read the labels.

Make a friend. Loneliness is a curse of our age. Think of someone having no family close by coming back to an empty house after a spell in hospital, not even being able to get on the bus to visit a friend. Think of someone who has fled persecution and become a refugee or asylum seeker, alone and stigmatised in a foreign country. A huge number of people are socially isolated and many charities run befriending networks that will try to match you up with someone who shares your interests. Befriending can mean just picking up the phone or writing a letter – it needn't be a huge commitment.

Share a meal. Ask someone you wouldn't normally socialise with to share a meal with you. I am not talking dinner parties and hard work. Quick, simple food – pasta, salad or hearty soup and cheese is fine. It's the company, conversation and friendship that's the most important thing. The very fact that you cared enough to ask them round.

Pop by. There will be someone you know who's unwell. Maybe depressed. Or just alone. Or stuck at home with a sick child – even just a young child. Make contact. If nothing else, ring them, and listen rather than talk. If you've time, arrange to visit. Taking flowers or a magazine is optional; it's your time that'll be valued.

Join a committee. I've deliberately left this till last. It's not for everyone, but communities need school governors and local parish councillors. Don't wait to be asked and don't moan on any longer about the pothole that hasn't been filled. Find out who to contact and put your name forward.

9

World Poverty

'If you can't feed a hundred people, then just feed one.'

Mother Teresa

You have the power

Clark Kent is a slightly geeky, mild-mannered reporter for the *Daily Planet* newspaper. Under the cover of this very ordinary life he lives another, as the ultimate hero Superman, possessing extraordinary powers – 'faster than a speeding bullet, more powerful than a locomotive, and able to leap tall buildings in a single bound'. He has superhuman strength, X-ray vision, super-hearing and the ability to run at amazing speeds, leap incredible distances and to fly.

He's been around since 1933, invented by Jerry Siegel and Joe Shuster, who were in turn inspired by heroes such as Samson and Hercules. The concept was to create a superhero who would right wrongs and fight for social justice and against tyranny.

'What is all this to do with me?' you ask. My guess is Superman's enduring appeal has something to do with an unspoken yearning to have a bit of Superman in ourselves. Let's assume for a moment that most of us have ordinary jobs that pay the bills and that we ask ourselves from time to time whether there is more to life. The message is: there *is*! We all have the ability to shed our ordinary lives, if only for a short while, put on our Superman outfits and do something that will right a few wrongs.

We can have much more fun and add meaning to life when we look for the superhero opportunities rather than wait for them to come to us. We all have the power to achieve extraordinary things, beyond the imagination of most people.

By 'most people' I am referring to the very poorest people in the world; the 'bottom billion' who live on the edge of life in extreme poverty, on less than $1 a day.

By contrast you already have superhuman powers – the ability to fight for social justice and human rights and save lives. Today. And to paraphrase Mother Teresa, if you can't help a billion, there's no reason not to help just one.

Time to show up

Procrastination isn't excusable. It is time to show up in life, grab the opportunity and make a real difference. You can save the life of an African child by giving them food and medicine today. Tomorrow will be too late. International travellers protect themselves against malaria, but this is still the biggest killer in Africa and can be prevented at minimal cost. You can provide education for an orphan or a street child so they have a chance to escape poverty and lift generations of their family away from a life of hunger and disease. You can actively support and provide funds for organisations that fight for human rights – reducing sex trafficking, child labour, slavery and torture.

It's just a drop in the pond ... No, it's not! To the child saved, the orphan educated or the tortured prisoner released – the starfish saved – you will quite simply be a hero. A real-life Superman – or -woman – using your own extraordinary powers:

intelligence, money and even bloody-minded determination, to improve the lives of your fellow human beings.

THE RIPPLE EFFECT OF ONE SMALL ACT: HILDE'S STORY

Hilde Back is a Holocaust survivor who came to live in Sweden after the war. She settled and became a teacher living a modest life, but she never forgot the kindness of the strangers who had welcomed her when she had first arrived, young and traumatised, her parents having been murdered.

She decided she wanted to help someone as well, so paid the secondary school fees for a young Kenyan whose parents couldn't afford them. It cost her $15 a month. The student, Chris Mburu, went on to graduate from Harvard and is today a United Nations human rights lawyer based in Switzerland.

As a boy, Chris's image of Hilde was that she must be rich. She, for her part, didn't know the huge difference she'd made to his life. And it was not until Chris decided to 'pay it forward' that he tracked her down in Sweden and realised that she was certainly not rich, just caring. And she did what she could. In 2001, he named the Hilde Back Education Fund in her honour. It provides scholarship funding for some of the brightest Kenyan students who can't afford secondary school fees. Their story has been told in the award-winning film *A Small Act*. As Chris says, 'I would like these kids to be educated ... because once you have a society that is very, very ignorant, it becomes the breeding ground for violence ... for intolerance.'

Hilde has the final word: 'If you do something good, it can spread in circles, like rings on the water.'

We are all supposed to be global citizens, in the sense that we live in an ever more interconnected world. Many of us have travelled to places our parents only dreamt about. With a couple of webcams, an internet connection and Skype, it costs nothing to chat face-to-face for hours to someone on the other side of the world. Basic computers with internet access and a screen that's readable in the bright sunlight of an outdoor classroom are available for a little over $200. Solar, mobile and wind technology are reducing dependence on non-existent electricity. YouTube, Facebook and Twitter, Pinterest, Instagram and more have enabled – for good or bad – images to be shared with millions. Smartphones connect people outside any electric grid.

Our access to world news is 24/7 and anyone reading this has the resources to source information worldwide in seconds. Being so easily informed, we can choose to engage and help people in other parts of the world quickly and instantly if we want to. It is surprisingly simple to be generous and to spread generosity.

Before you say, 'Yes, but I don't have the time to check this all out,' here are a few stats.

Live simply that others may simply live

The World Bank defines extreme poverty as not having enough income to meet the most basic human needs for food, water, shelter, clothing, sanitation, health care and education. The latest numbers were calculated in 2011, when 14.5 per cent of the global population was estimated to be living on less than $1.25 per day. Over 40 per cent of this number lived in 'fragile and conflict-affected situations'.

Refugee stats come from UNHCR and are more recent. To quote: 'During the year, conflict and persecution forced an average of 32,200 persons per day to leave their homes and seek refuge elsewhere.' The year they are referring to is 2013, when the numbers of displaced people increased by 1.2 million to 16.7 million. Global stability hasn't improved since then, so the trend continues. The desperate migration of families fleeing Syria, Afghanistan, Eritrea and other war-torn, chaotic countries makes daily headlines.

It's one of the conundrums of the world we live in. Poverty is very often at the root of conflict and conflict drags ever more innocent people into a life where education is a luxury, nutrition is basic and life is on hold. Many of today's refugees have abandoned homes and livelihoods that supported their family life. So whilst poverty reduction initiatives make some progress, refugee numbers grow in tandem. The overall number doesn't seem to change – a little over a billion people from our global population of seven billion live with a daily struggle to feed themselves, including many who are displaced. I, personally, cannot visualise a million people, let alone a billion. But, as journalists know, it is the pictures and stories of individuals that get through to us.

Famine, not just hunger

'We imagine that 'famine' is being hungry and thirsty, but when you go to a famine area you realise the complete nothingness and emptiness of famine – it is truly unimaginable. There is no reason to wake up, no reason to be up, nothing to do once you are up, no activity, no energy, nothing to sit on – everything has been sold – no animals; you just wake up and sometime later you go back to sleep. There is ... absolutely ... nothing, complete emptiness – soul and spirit drained.'

David Gold, founder, A Glimmer of Hope, Ethiopia

About 21,000 people are dying of hunger every day. The most vulnerable are the children who, malnourished and without treatment, can't fight diarrhoea, malaria and other common viruses. Count slowly to four seconds and know another hungry person has died. Someone's mother, father, daughter or son. For a sobering reminder go to Make Poverty History (www.makepovertyhistory.org) and watch one of their short videos.

A minute is fifteen deaths. The best way to grasp this, or rather begin to get it, is to click your fingers and count four seconds, then click again. Each click marks another death. If you're a quick reader, around 200 people will have died in the time it takes to read this chapter.

By contrast, the World Health Organization is monitoring our health at the other end of the scale and the number of over-weight people (1.9 billion) is now almost double that of those starving. Most are from 'the developed world'. As mentioned in Chapter 5, half the food we buy is wasted between the plough and the plate; 30 per cent is thrown away. The amount of food thrown out each year in North America and Europe is enough to feed the world's hungriest people three times over.

It is incredibly easy to glaze over when people start reeling out numbers like these. But the fact remains that in an hour's time almost a thousand people will have died of starvation, while a thousand people living near you overeat, or throw away enough food to have fed them.

Those dying are in another country, only intruding in our lives through news reports or documentaries. Our lives are already stressful enough, we all think: we are working, trying to lose weight, fitting in visits to the gym or Weight Watchers; day-to-day living takes up most of our attention. Our focus, totally naturally, is on our own needs first. It is so easy to turn our backs on people who live out their lives in another country, another culture – but it is also grotesque. We can no longer bury our heads in the sand and pretend we live in unconnected isolation. The life choices you and I make ripple outwards. While one part of the world is expecting reduced life expectancy brought about by obesity, in another part of the world fellow human beings starve to death.

If this is where 'survival of the fittest' takes us, we need to set off in another direction. To quote the cartoonist Bill Watterson, 'Sometimes I think that the surest sign that intelligent life exists in other worlds is that no one has tried to contact us.'

Aliens living in their more advanced worlds and star systems presumably look at their version of Sky News in the evening, enter 'Earth' on their remote controls and stare in disbelief at man's inhumanity to man.

It may be that future generations, too, will look back on this time and regard our behaviour as a crime against humanity, in much the same way as we now look back on slavery. It took William Wilberforce forty years to get Parliament to abolish slavery. His fight was mostly against the commercial interests of the day, which were heavily reliant on slave labour. He gave his life to the abolition of slavery, but success came at another price. The Slave Trade Act was passed only when a sum equivalent to £20 million in today's values was paid to compensate landowners and businessmen.

In the twenty-first century, more than half of the world's largest economies are not countries but commercial enterprises. And they still live by certain rules: profit before people, because that's the model – it's what shareholders demand.

Perhaps our challenges are not so different to those of Mr Wilberforce.

'We live in an age when the consequences of our decisions seem less and less important, because we don't really know

what they are. We 'love a bargain' but don't see the appalling
conditions endured by the people who produce a product that
can be sold so cheaply. We troop to the supermarket but don't
see the small businesses and farmers whose livelihoods are
wrecked by 'everyday low prices'. The human consequences
of our decisions are felt by people separated from us by time,
space, and class.'

Steve Hilton, policy advisor and author

Climate change

Climate change is making the eradication of poverty increasingly
difficult. Most of the world's poorest people live in places that
are extremely vulnerable to global warming. Heat is a killer.
When the seasons change and the rains don't come, crops fail.
When the rains pour, mud-built buildings are washed away
and there are few, if any, resources to store water, with rainfall
becoming increasingly heavy and erratic.

In January 2014, after extended heavy rain, flooding affected
the Somerset Levels in England. Six hundred homes were
affected, kids weren't able to get to school, villages were cut off,
herds of cattle had to be moved and the story dominated the
UK news. In August 2014, over 500,000 people were left homeless in Bangladesh after flash flooding. The *Wall Street Journal*
spoke to a farmer by phone: 'I've lost my home and my rice.
My two cows are also missing. I don't know how I'll survive the
year.' The poorest suffer more than we do.

In January 2015, over 170,000 people were displaced and
60,000 hectares of crops destroyed when unprecedented floods
hit Malawi. Did you know or care?

'It's all a waste of time'

No doubt you can reel off a whole load of reasons why you have decided not to act. Like most people, you probably doubt that you could make any difference. And you justify this with the usual excuses: 'Charity begins at home'; 'All overseas governments are corrupt'; 'Most of the money goes on 4x4s, five-star hotels and administration'; 'The money never gets through to the people who really need it'.

But you are wrong. The people working in most aid agencies do outstanding work. Remember Mother Teresa, and the starfish story too – one life saved *is* worthwhile. It would be to you if it were your life.

Some governments are corrupt, but this is not solely an African sport. Western democracies are heavily infiltrated and influenced by lobbying firms and have their fair share of scandals; financial, personal and political. We are interconnected by our humanity and our failings. Some aid is inefficient and some incredibly efficient, especially if you stick with it.

I have often observed that those with the most definite and unchallengeable views on this topic have the least knowledge – and no desire to learn more, much less go on a field trip to find out. They are just 'right'. Perhaps some of them simply want an excuse for not giving when they never actually had any intention of giving anyway.

Luckily, most of us are not like that. In 2015 Comic Relief broke the magic £1 billion for funds raised over 30 years. We're generous in an emergency. The British public donated £34 million in three months to deal with ebola in Sierra Leone. We responded to the typhoon in the Philippines in November 2013 by donating £94 million. The rebuilding programme that money financed runs until 2016. With over 4 million people displaced, and homes, fishing boats and crops destroyed, the whole infrastructure of that nation needed support.

Every year millions of people from the diaspora populations of the world send money back home to support their families and friends. The term used is 'remittances'. Individuals send three times more money back home than is provided by global aid budgets and the money transferred has tripled in a decade. So people helping people informally spread more global wealth than NGOs and government aid combined. The money goes directly to whoever needs it, and as someone with huge experience in this field said, 'It's nearly all for health, education and basic needs and if some of it buys a bottle of whisky, so what? At least it's supporting the local economy.'

Roughly 41 per cent of the Somali population rely on the lifeline they get from remittances – an amount equal to over half of Somalia's gross national income. It's worth repeating. An amount larger than all the aid from governments around the world is coming from individuals choosing to even up the inequality between their lives and the lives of those they care about, with who knows what ripple effect. And I'm willing to bet that the majority sending money back home aren't living high-rolling lifestyles themselves.

The diaspora communities already do a huge amount. As for the rest of us, we trust the major aid agencies to co-ordinate and prioritise, to get our donations to where they are needed most. We put our hands in our pockets in response to massive media coverage and because the need is so obvious. Even the harshest critics of development aid support aid for emergencies.

This is all great, of course, but you don't have to wait for a disaster that makes headlines or for Bono or Bob Geldof to appeal to your better side in order to be generous. You could be generous today.

The wrong sort of aid

In fairness to the gloom merchants, let's acknowledge that nothing is perfect. Not all aid is well-directed or appropriate, and disastrous mistakes have been made in the past.

In the best of all possible worlds, what works best is when we help people to help themselves. It takes patience to work with people who don't live their lives with funders' outputs and outcomes in mind. And much more than patience when there's a whole culture that needs to shift, as a highly respected Indian philanthropist told me. 'You have to understand,' he murmured gently to me in our meeting, 'that there are two Cs in India: caste and corruption.

'And, of course,' he went on, 'the most sought-after job in India is that of a civil servant in a regional government. They get paid for doing their job, handing out money as directed by central government, and they get paid by the people they're handing the money out to. It's good for them, no? To be paid twice.' And despite the efforts of the current Indian prime minister, who has taken a high-profile stance against a system that seems to be endemically corrupt, there is still, even if you're an optimist, a very long way to go.

---

365 WAYS TO CHANGE THE WORLD: MICHAEL'S STORY

Michael Norton is a practical, hands-on type. He has founded several successful NGOs and written numerous books, the most interesting and entertaining of which is *365 Ways to Change the World: How to Make a Better World Every Day*.

Michael has been proactively involved with Indian and African NGOs for many years. He is not a fan of aid agencies. In his view they become arrogant, treat people – even their donors – badly and turn into outcome machines, where the outcomes are promised but never really delivered.

Michael illustrated his point with a story about a visit to a village in Uganda with the head of a large, well-known overseas NGO. The boss was a well-meaning guy who spent most of his working hours in an office with a team of very bright and educated Africans, compiling reports for overseas donors. When they arrived at the village the head man presented them with a list of 34 things that they would like funded.

Michael asked for the list to be read out, one item at a time. After each, he asked three questions.

- Is this something you could do by yourselves entirely?
- Do you need a little bit of help?
- Do you need a lot of help?

Of the 34 requests, 27 were jobs the villagers either needed no help with at all or only a little, leaving 7 where the NGO was *really* needed. Yet in ordinary circumstances, the NGO would simply have approved the list, and ticked them off as successful 'outcomes'. It was a classic case of learned dependency.

'The development agencies' role is to empower communities,' Michael explained, 'yet this community was sitting there not doing anything. The development programmes weren't changing life much anyway, and what they wanted they could mostly do themselves. And if you learn to do the easy things yourselves, or with a little help, you're more able to cope with the more difficult ones later.'

And even when not arrogant, agencies are often beholden to their funders. All that might be needed is a few bus fares to allow a group of women in Afghanistan to meet up and begin to address local issues together, but a bus fare isn't the 'measurable outcome' needed to keep the donors happy and so the women don't meet and the expensive 'monitoring and evaluation' industry just grows.

We are the problem, not them

It can often seem that what starts as a genuine desire to help gets lost at every stage. It's incredibly difficult for our Department for International Development (DFID) to gauge what will work best at a micro level in a country with a different culture. In addition, governments deal with governments, and we know from our own experience that bureaucratic procedures are rarely effective, even before we take corruption into account. NGOs should, and often do, perform better, but they also bid for funding from DFID and the EU, so a culture can develop in which somewhere along the line we leave our instincts and our common sense behind.

If funding depends on outcomes and targets which have been agreed in advance in an office somewhere, quite often in a different country, people will say whatever their sponsors want to hear to get hold of the cash, and bias their reports back for success, whatever the actual outcome. But this leads to ever more stringent controls and an increasing cycle of reporting requirements, with almost as much energy put into trying to monitor the results as into the aid in the first place.

For something to succeed, it needs to be generated by the people, with the people and for the people. We need to *listen*. We need to trust them to get on with it. They need to trust us. We need to stop being patronising. It's no different from changing the communities we live in ourselves. *Bottom-up works. Change takes time.*

Aid tourism

If it takes an anthropologist a couple of years to start to understand a culture properly, what hope is there for a visiting Oxbridge
graduate who doesn't speak the language? I've come across too
many stories of disillusioned gap-year travellers who confirm tales
of overseas aid workers living the life of Riley in former colonial
outposts and of projects clustered round international airports
for ease of access. The daftest story involved the donation of a
reindeer from a Scandinavian charity to an Ethiopian village, at
absurd cost and with a predictably unhappy outcome.

More common are tales of abandoned wells, rusting vehicles
and failed tree plantations. These situations often come about
for the simplest of reasons: lack of training, use of inappropriate
materials, failure to provide or fund spare parts. Even simply the
enthusiasm of funding something tangible waning in the face of
the difficulty of keeping it going.

Keeping it going can often be a struggle. When overseas NGOs
recruit local staff, they pay above-average salaries, attracting the
best talent – until the funding runs out. Local NGOs, who in the
meantime have struggled to recruit, are left to pick up the pieces
when the international aid agency withdraws.

As they say their goodbyes, they cite their excuses. Priorities
have changed. The focus is now elsewhere.

The right sort of aid

It doesn't need to be like this. And, in the main, it isn't. We have
learnt from the past – sometimes even from the distant past,
as when Oxfam built an incredibly successful campaign on an
ancient Chinese proverb: 'Give a man a fish and you feed him for
a day, teach a man to fish and you feed him for a lifetime.' We're

now encouraged to give a chicken or a goat, with the potential for eggs, milk, biofuels and the whole village economy, not just a meal.

Michael Norton is again worth paying attention to when he says that: 'You can't do things *to* people. You can't really do things *for* people. For example, you can't teach a child who doesn't want to learn. People will only really change if they learn to help themselves. You can only do things *with* people. Working to encourage them to do things themselves.'

The best aid agencies have learned how to do this. When there is trust, they can ask open-ended questions and get honest answers. 'What do you most need?'– an open question, asked by someone who had worked a long time in the slums in Bangladesh of a woman there. The answer? 'A private place for the women to shower.' Hardly a headline for a fundraising ad. Behind the answer, though, lay the knowledge that without it the women, all Muslim, were getting up at 3 a.m. (before the men were around) to wash at the public pump. It doesn't take long for the penny to drop about the impact of sleep deprivation on half the adult population of the slum and their ability to live a decent life and maintain their dignity. But it is not a priority I, personally, would have thought of.

'I'LL FLY TO THE MOON WITH YOU': JULIA'S STORY

Julia Lalla-Maharajh, is the founder and CEO of the Orchid Project, a small charity with the big ambition of ending female genital mutilation (FGM) worldwide. Julia is one of those people who has followed her heart and found she's always been in the right place at the right time – even if she didn't know it. She has learnt that working for change takes patience and time, because what is needed is trust. The more you trust people, the more they help you. Yes, it is not without risk, but risk is an integral part of life.

'My Damascene moment was in Lalibela, Ethiopia: a beautiful place of pilgrimage for over 1,000 years, where churches had been cut into the rock.

'I was working on an educational project for VSO at the time, living with an Ethiopian family. Reading *Lonely Planet* one month in, some words jumped off the page. "A scream so strong it would shake the very earth." The article was by a doctor about FGM and she was emphasising its widespread nature by writing that if all the girls who had experienced FGM screamed together, the earth would shake.

'I'd known about FGM for many years; 75 per cent of the girls in Ethiopia were cut. Suddenly, it became important to me.

'How do you talk about a taboo? I started to seek out activists; I needed legitimacy as an outsider. Everyone said it was a human rights issue and if I were the sort of person who would join Amnesty, I could do something about FGM. My head told me this was awful, a mutilation, but my heart told me that I lived with and knew Ethiopian families who loved their daughters. I couldn't understand why they would willingly harm them. It was too difficult and I chose to look away.

'It was in Lalibela I met the girls who changed my life. Two little girls of about five or six, selling trinkets. They were lively and joyous and I was sure they hadn't been cut. Could I save them? I'd talk to their parents, pay for their education, support them, change their lives. But at the same time I knew it was hopeless. I couldn't rescue them. I lacked the language. Why should they introduce me to their parents anyway?

'As I walked away I took the photo I still keep in my wallet. I was devastated, but I made a vow to do what I could to help end FGM and I pledged to myself that I would.

'Back in London I was running out of money trying to get something going which just wasn't happening. Then, on 20 December 2009, a friend emailed me a link to a YouTube competition. "Make a three-minute film about an urgent human rights issue to win a platform at the World Economic Forum at Davos in January." One last shot. I roped in a film-maker friend and on Christmas Eve we put the film together and met the year-end deadline.

'Early in January I got the call telling me I was a finalist, could I clear the next two weeks?

'The final hurdle was to reach out to my networks and get the most votes to win. Every friend, friends of friends and friends of theirs helped run a two-week campaign round a kitchen table. This is an issue that cannot be marginalised. It's not just about the women; it's an economic and social issue that affects everyone.

'Competition closed, I went for a walk and returned to a missed call ... I'd won a dedicated panel discussion at Davos, with six days to prepare.

'So began my second life. Six days to think up a name, put a website together, print business cards, film a daily YouTube diary (part of the deal) and get a haircut, not to mention buying snow boots.

'Davos was extraordinary. I learnt that the only way to begin to break a taboo is to speak about it. No pussy-footing. You need to use very straight language. Evan Davis tweeted: 'Just met a woman talking about vaginas at WEF and she's doing a great job.' But when they asked, 'What can I do?' I didn't know. Michael Halbye, CEO of McKinsey, suggested I might like to come to his fiftieth birthday party in Denmark. A hundred and seventy of Michael's close friends were invited with 'no presents but I'm going to introduce you to three charities. Please help them if you can'.

'More outfits, an amazing gathering, but Michael is Danish, all his friends are Danish, and the other two charities presented in Danish. Presenting blind, I still got twenty people wanting to help; wanting clarity and business plans I didn't have. Until someone spoke up: "I get it. You want to fly to the moon." A shiver went up my spine. "I'll fly to the moon with you."

'Through Davos I'd an introduction to Molly Melching. She'd set up a charity called Tostan, working to reduce FGM in Senegal. Molly challenged me to think about where change happens. The answer is obvious to me now, but wasn't then. Communities are at the heart of change and Tostan's community programme in Senegal was stopping FGM. As one man told me when I visited later: 'People have come for years and told us not to do this, but this programme has taught me to reach for a higher good.' Dialogue is based on trust, respect, compassion, empathy and understanding. That was the way forward.'

'I worked out my plan. There'd be a coalition of influential organisations with leverage to galvanise change and we would still be utterly committed to a bottom-up, grass-roots programme that would have legitimacy. DFID was impossible to get through to. I tried for six months. "Who are you? Oh, two people ..." No response from anyone. FGM was nowhere on their agenda at all.

'Life is amazing. We accepted free space in a slightly dubious part of Victoria. An empty retail unit in a dingy street with a large shop window. We used it to put up a picture telling the story of FGM and its impact. Then one of my mates mentioned he knew someone from DFID who'd probably agree to a coffee. When we met, she suddenly asked, 'Are you the person behind that big shop window round the corner?' My drab and dingy street was the cut-through between Victoria station and the DFID. The DFID office talk was about tactical guerrilla marketing! That was another breakthrough.'

Today, the Orchid Project, the charity Julia founded in 2011, has helped secure £35 million of DFID funding to end FGM worldwide.

'I've met and talked to incredibly inspiring people who live life with their heart and heads – Desmond Tutu, Graça Machel, Malala Yousafzai, villagers in rural communities in Somalia, Senegal, Gambia ... Orchid works in a way that is congruent with our values, ethos, passion and purpose. We are using our heads, but have a big dose of heart with it. My anchor is that I know that people are fundamentally good. There are huge challenges but we can and are ending FGM.'

Trust and risk

So the challenge for many of us is to reconfigure how we think about a more sustainable global family. Listening requires generosity of thought. The leader of a major aid agency wisely remarked to me that poor people, from the slums of Delhi to the rural villages of Africa, don't introduce themselves as poor. They don't walk up to you and say, 'Hi, my name is Sanjay and I am poor.' They are living their own lives with dignity. We need to be prepared to respect the culture and values of an Ethiopian herdsman or an Amazonian hunter and accept that they have as much validity as our own. We, in the developed world, are not a super-intelligent race with all the answers.

It is only by listening that we come to understand and, over time, build trust. It is only by listening that we realise there is no silver bullet that is going to change things overnight, or in a decade. Life is complex and societies are in constant flux. Communities are a bit like a delicate house of cards. With all the cards in place, there is balance; remove one and the house may collapse. We need to focus on hearing the messages we receive direct from the bottom billion, addressing the power imbalance, reducing our impact on them by caring about climate change, recognising that our motivations have been shaped not only by our culture and our media, but also by vested commercial interests.

> *'Go to the people,*
> *Live with them, learn from them*
> *Love them.*
> *Start with what they know*
> *Build with what they have*
> *But of the best leaders*
> *When their job is done*
> *The task accomplished*
> *The people will say*
> *"We have done it ourselves."'*
>
> Lao Tzu, Chinese philosopher

We need to stop thinking we know best – and that solutions need to be delivered in a year or two to deserve our funding. Systemic change takes time. With access to the internet and a bit of time for research, any individual can find examples of development aid that work, are proven and sustainable. We can find aid agencies that are committed to listening and empowering local, long-term change. And then we can join them, so we're all doing something about it.

Microcredit for beginners

Microcredit hit the world's consciousness in 2006, when the Nobel Peace Prize was jointly awarded to Muhammad Yunus and the Grameen Bank which he founded in 1983.

Their innovation solved an age-old problem which would still endure but for microcredit. The problem is that when you are poor you have no collateral, are deemed too high-risk for established lenders and end up being sucked dry by loan sharks or denied any sort of finance at all. Yunus's analogy for people who are poor is that they are 'Bonsai people'. A tree seed planted in a small pot will never grow tall, although there's nothing wrong with it at all. Likewise, society doesn't create the environment for the poorest people to flourish. Through Grameen, Yunus established a bank whose sole aim was to lend money to poor families, particularly groups of women, and so help them to set up their own small businesses. He believed he could unleash their potential and help them out of poverty by giving them access to finance and training.

The loans are usually tiny (hence 'micro'credit); $50 can be enough to get someone started and the average loan is just a little over $100. They are always unsecured and made to groups of at least five people. The group may weave or sew or open a market stall together, and no one wants to let the others down – they share the responsibility, and success or failure is a communal achievement. Grameen now has 8.4 million customers in 44 countries, 97 per cent of whom are women. The repayment rate on the loans is a completely staggering 97 per cent, something beyond the dreams of our high-street banks. Grameen understands that people want to help themselves and can. The initial concept has now become multiple strong organisations, with the Grameen Foundation establishing Bankers Without Borders, using talented professional volunteers to coach, train and transfer their skills. And they take donations.

Barclays, RBS, *et al.*, eat your hearts out. It is nothing short of amazing that simply lending money to the poorest people on the planet gives them the opportunity to create their own small businesses, lift themselves out of poverty by their own efforts and repay the loans entirely.

It seems there's always a battle between profit and altruism. Microfinance has become a developing industry, but it's buyer beware. Low-cost commercial microcredit businesses keep interest rates attractive by cutting out most of the core elements so essential to success. Money often goes to centres that distribute it to men not groups of women; the training so vital for a small business to succeed isn't available and when people create products no one wants to buy they soon need another loan to pay off the first. Revolving credit, despair and mistrust of the whole system follows.

In this internet age, anyone, in any country, can engage directly in microfinance, but it can be difficult to establish which schemes are really effective. All the bigger organisations work with local partners, whom they need to monitor closely. Fraud can be an issue. How tempting to take the money raised abroad and siphon off a little for yourself. And taking legal action in a developing country is anything but easy, especially when no bribes are on offer.

Kiva (www.kiva.org) was set up in 2005 and is one of the most established microfinance charities linking the public with locally based agencies who introduce budding village entrepreneurs. Kiva believes in publishing bad news as well as good, including telling supporters when they drop local partners because of fraud. Kiva's founder, Matt Flannery, benchmarked his decisions by asking himself, 'Would you be proud if your actions were described on the front page of the *New York Times*?' As Kiva has continued to grow, its due diligence and monitoring is much more stringent than in the early years. It has now distributed over $750 million in loans to over 1.3 million small businesses.

Kiva suggests lending $25 for starters. Donations are pooled behind the scenes, but you'll be helping someone make great strides towards economic independence to create an improved life for themselves, their family and their community. Throughout the course of the loan (usually 6–12 months) you can receive email journal updates and track repayments. Then, with the loan repaid, many choose to recycle it by lending the money to someone else. The Kiva repayment rate is 98.75 per cent and they support people in 83 countries.

You'll have spotted it already, but the principle of microfinance is that it is small, personal and gets directly through to people who have previously been the prey of loan sharks. It works by bringing people together to support communities that want to change themselves. Its impact is bottom-up. And, at the same time, it is an industry with a great track record. Microfinance organisations monitor results, know what works and share that knowledge. However dubious you might have been about the power you have to change things for the world's bottom billion, this one definitely works.

BEING TRUSTED TO LIFT THE VERY, VERY POOREST OUT OF POVERTY: OLLY'S STORY

Olly is one of my heroes. She could have forged a high-flying career in practically any sphere she chose but has made it her personal mission to help the very, very poorest in West Bengal. She originally set up Shivia as a microfinance charity, raising money in the UK and working with local Indian and Nepalese partners to deliver interest-free loans. Olly knows the countries well and had studied the issues, but what seemed relatively straightforward initially is now very different.

A key catalyst was the growth of profit-driven microfinance in India. Families received little support or training. They were being offered loans to weave items or make jewellery they couldn't sell, then had to take further loans to pay back the original ones. Olly felt she needed her own team in India to ensure financial and management control as well as shared values.

So she quietly regrouped and went through all the hoops to establish her own delivery charity in Bengal: Nirdhan (Shivia India), funded by Shivia UK. A year was spent on research: what enterprises would suit the very poorest? What can women do from home that they can sell? If they can't sell it, will they be able to use it anyway? What would involve the whole family? (If you just target women their men don't like it.) Olly was determined to find businesses that really involved and supported women.

The Nirdhan Poultry Toolkits have now been refined over four years. Over 35,000 people have been trained in poultry farming. Raising chicks is something everyone in the family can help with. Each starter toolkit includes ten one-day-old chicks (or ducklings for better survival rates during the monsoon season), feed, vaccinations and six months of training for a subsidised cost of £5. The regional government had given out chicks before but without the knowledge of how to rear them, most died, so a poultry business wasn't an easy sell. There's a coop to build, then lights to power to keep the chicks warm in winter, shade to create to give protection from the summer heat, plus owners need to ensure protection from fowl pox, snakes and rats.

'Poultry provides the very poorest with a stepping stone,' says Olly. 'Some use the money to mend their husband's rickshaw. Others have set up roadside stalls selling omelettes and tea; some trade chickens or eggs for veg. We've also asked what else we could do. Some have a tiny plot of inherited land but no idea what to do with it; 500 families have paid £1 (again subsidised) to have the soil tested for advice on what will grow, how to make the land productive and cultivate the crops. Rice, mustard and brindle feed the family and can be sold as well. We group the farmers into interest groups, and they elect a treasurer and president to buy seed wholesale.

'The very poorest don't have land; many are Muslim immigrants who aren't allowed to lease land or even given access to water. How could we help them? We're now in the middle of piloting goat farming. In Bengal, goats are known as the "asset of the poor". With goats as collateral you *can* access water; you earn respect as a member of the community, so you can borrow because you have a goat. Nirdhan own the male goats and the families are given females that produce a couple of kids a year.

'What we do is driven locally. Logistics can be a nightmare. There's a huge amount of legwork involved in getting the different licences we need to operate, all of which need renewing every year; in making sure the suppliers don't let us down and that the chicks are delivered on the right day; in negotiating the best price for the kits (each costs £15); in keeping the chicks alive; winning the trust of the clients at every level is vital. Our field staff are all local. Most come from families where no one has had a job. They're always out there, they know all the clients, so over and above our official impact monitoring they can see if a child has shoes and is going to school and, of course, the women like to talk. Domestic violence is down. Husbands and sons respect them more and the kids see their mum working. Chandrani, our head of operations, sums it up well:'

We can try and measure our impact through data collection and analysis but, ultimately, the smiles of the people say it all. They are no longer smiles of hope but smiles of achievement, no longer smiles with resignation in their eyes, but smiles with twinkles in their eyes.

How one cappuccino can change the world

Small, local, direct. Generosity starts with knowing that we can trust people to help themselves. We know microfinance and remittances work. We know that aid agencies that listen find better solutions. Development is changing and our attitudes need to change as well, recognising that quality of life is not directly proportional to material comforts and that relatively low-cost interventions can have amazing ripple effects. Another example from David Gold, founder of Ethiopian charity A Glimmer of Hope:

> 'We walked to the water well that is within the community and does not require the women to spend hours every day walking and queuing for water; usually carrying back-breaking pots. This well was hand-dug to a depth of 15 to 20 metres and with the equipment had cost $2,000. The well serves a community of approximately 500 people. The simple calculation is stunning: $4 per person for life. For the price of a cappuccino, a human being gets access to clean water for the rest of their life.'

The immediate benefit of the well is obvious: clean drinking water. However, the power of the well is incredible and goes way beyond that. David listed the other benefits:

- Less time needed to collect water; and therefore the women spend more time in their community and on education, health and other community activities
- School enrolment rate amongst younger women improves
- Sharp decrease in falls and accidents and illness
- Reduction in miscarriages
- Nutritional status improves as the women have more time to spend on food preparation

- Reduction in diarrhoeal diseases – by as much as 65 per cent
- Overall improvement in health care
- Body and clothes are washed far more frequently so there are fewer fleas and bugs that carry disease

All of this is a 'forever' step change that fundamentally improves people's lives – for not much more than the price of a bottle of Evian. It is not rocket science, nor hugely difficult to understand. It is just common sense. This is the true work of a Superman or -woman – of any one of us – for just $4.

We have the knowledge and the resources, practical and financial, to lift the bottom billion out of poverty. The UN has made the first of its development goals for 2030 to 'end poverty in all its forms everywhere'. We simply need the will to do so. Set yourself a personal goal – even if it's only to do something a couple of times a year.

OVERWHELMED BY THE PEOPLE OF BLESSED BRANCH: DAVID'S STORY

Philanthropist David Gold was making an unannounced and unplanned stop at an Ethiopian village, rather appropriately called Blessed Branch. The visitors entered on foot, vehicles parked out of sight. In his own words:

'The village was clearly poor, with people living in mud huts. The villagers only had access to appalling water miles away, because the Italians had built a reservoir in the wrong place. People used the reservoir to wash their cars in, so the water was full of oil.

'The villagers were living off goats' milk. I asked them what they did if they ever had surplus milk and have never forgotten their answer. "We give it to poor people." I was stunned; they

206

"give it to poor people" – they live almost entirely off goats' milk, and if they have a surplus, they don't take it to markets, they "give it to poor people".

'We had a football with us, which we gave them, and the entire village and all of the people from A Glimmer of Hope were playing football together. They gave us everything. They played with us and they partied with us and they talked with us – and there was nothing in it for them. They didn't do it because they expected something from us – I was overwhelmed with their generosity.'

Develop your Generous Gene

Keep an open mind. Recognise that the starving people whose pictures you see on the television news are not living on another planet, they are living on *our* planet. It is almost certain that our greed – and that of those who exploit the developing world's mineral and other natural resources – has contributed to the drought that made their crops fail and their cattle die. Recognise, too, that commercial interests lobby politicians and spend heavily on PR to feed the media. The scales are not balanced, especially in global markets.

Learn the facts. Motivate yourself to learn more about world poverty and how you can be the change. Listen to the small voices as well as the major change-makers' voices. Discover grass-roots projects by checking out www.justgiving.com, www.globalgiving.co.uk and www.givewell.org, or hear from charities directly by going to an event run by The Funding Network (www.thefundingnetwork.org.uk).

Find out what works. It is more sensible to find out what's working than try to reinvent the wheel. That is what Grameen,

Kiva and Shivia do. Examples might include: sand dams that raise the level of the water table for miles around, which in turn changes the local micro-climate; biofuel projects – a few chickens or pigs provide manure, which becomes fuel for heat and electricity, which means evenings are lit after sunset so kids can do their homework; eco toilets that can be built by local communities for as little as £20, reducing ill health in an entire community.

Spend less of your holiday on the beach. Build time into your long-haul holiday to visit a local charity and plan it ahead. Stay overnight if it's appropriate and possible. Include your kids. Children are a great ice-breaker, and the impact on them of seeing other kids with huge grins on their faces and joining in football games with bamboo-woven balls will stay with them forever. If you like what you see, take a risk, really listen to what they need and become Superman. Challenge your assumptions while you're there. Seeing kids showering in the open under hoses in a Kerala orphanage, our guide noticed my face. 'We set up the showers like this on purpose. It's what the kids are used to in the villages and are most at ease with here.'

Be the change. If we put our minds to it, we can all raise sufficient money to fund the salary of a teacher in a school in a developing country for a year – it's just a few hundred pounds. £400 can fund a water-catchment tank in the Rajasthan desert. £1,000 will build a well. Search out first people you can trust to know where the real priorities lie. Stick with it. Changing lives cannot be rushed. You will have the satisfaction of seeing small changes become large over time. Dipping in and out doesn't help a child who needs long-term education or a village that can't fund a spare part for their well. Work with and learn from each other long term.

Twin your village. Or your Scout group or your faith group, with an African village community, or your school with an Indian orphanage or education project, or your town with an Asian town. The outside links and involvement and the opportunity to exchange visits, as well as providing access to a source of Western money and expertise, will create an impact beyond anything you first imagined.

Support a friend. My friend Hugh spent six months in India as a VSO teacher in his early twenties. Twenty years later, he returned to the village with his wife. Instantly recognisable (English, over 6 foot and blond), he was welcomed as a long-lost friend. What hit him hardest was the obvious. His life had moved on, he'd built a career, he was simply on holiday in another part of the world. But in the village, nothing had changed. He returned home, gave money, raised money, found the tax breaks and set up a school. Today, another twenty years on, that school educates over 1,000 children. And the village *has* changed. So find a friend who has a commitment to a long-term change project overseas and support them. It is easier to support someone you know is already doing great work than it is to start your own NGO!

Engage with an aid agency. Don't wait for an emergency appeal. Find an agency whose work makes you proud, one you admire and trust, or one your friends and colleagues speak highly of. Engage, become a trustee, raise funds, share your expertise. We are all in this together. Join the 4 million people already signed up to www.avaaz.org who are lobbying policy-makers world-wide and crowdfunding immediate and direct emergency aid to refugees and disaster-hit areas.

Become a microfinancier. Get involved with a small, personal and direct microfinance NGO like Shivia, or search Kiva for a selection of projects to co-fund, or help Grameen grow. www.shivia.com; www.kiva.org; www.grameenfoundation.org.

An Earth to Inherit

'We do not inherit the earth from our ancestors,
we borrow it from our children.'

Native American proverb

Living with climate change

F ew are still debating this: we are breathing in more carbon
dioxide than at any previous time in history; measuring
our oceans acidifying at a rate which is endangering the
micro-organisms and corals that live in them. Scientists ponder
the exact impact and the timeframe, but agree to a man and
woman, that our time is running out. Pope Francis and Barack
Obama are convinced as well. We are living with man-made
global warming and extreme weather conditions and going
rapidly beyond the point of no return – for humans and perhaps
even for our living planet. Scientific modelling beyond the
impact on people to the global impact of our changing climate,
ecosystems and rising sea levels isn't giving encouraging results.

Hats off to the *Guardian*'s outgoing editor-in-chief Alan
Rusbridger for his 2015 climate-change campaign 'Keep It in
the Ground'. The question he asked himself before launching
the campaign was what might he regret when stepping down
after 20 years at the helm? He made a decision to do all that
he could in his power to influence public opinion, corporations

and governments to keep fossil fuels in the ground. To stop the inexorable rise in CO2 emissions that will lead to disastrous global temperature increases of more than two degrees centigrade. We are currently on track for the planet's temperature to increase between three and four degrees centigrade by 2100. Globally, despite strong growth in green fuels and products, the investment in fossil fuels is much greater. 'Over £300 billion worth of oil "discovered" in Sussex!' shouts the headline, at the same time as calls emerge to 'protect our open countryside' from the 'blight' of solar panels and wind turbines and a government fast-tracks planning applications for fracking in the UK. Come on! What will be the legacy for today's children?

If I'm getting a bit evangelical about this, it's because it's so fundamental. You and I may not be scientists, we may think that nothing too drastic will happen to affect *us* in our lifetimes, but it is totally sensible and, yes, *generous* to think beyond ourselves for those who will come afterwards, rather than carry on with our heads in the sand.

One global climate-change summit after another has 'made progress' whilst failing to put global interests before self-interests. How short-sighted can we be? How much more evidence do we need before we have the conversation which acknowledges that we breathe the same air, drink the same water, share the same finite resources? Sacrificing our environment to the altar of economic development makes no sense. It's not rocket science. We just need to act.

Climate-change summits come round like clockwork. Almost as predictable are the world leaders calling for the courage to make difficult commitments – to put our mutual self-interest before that of individual political agendas – to collaborate. Put simply, to create a world fit for everyone to share in 2100. What's not to like about that? By being generous to everyone, the world is more stable, with fewer living life on the edge. The worrying news is that as yet those world leaders haven't quite put their money where their soundbite-laden mouths are ...

'We are the first generation to understand the consequences of a high carbon economy on the planet, on future prosperity and, in particular, on the most vulnerable around the world. Let us be the generation that stands up and takes the responsibility conveyed by that knowledge.'

Christiana Figueres, executive secretary,
UN Framework Convention on Climate Change

Of course it is the poorest who suffer most from global warming. The crowded delta of Bangladesh, the low-lying, unprotected islands in the Indian and Pacific Oceans come readily to mind. But what about the knock-on impact of people who are displaced across the world by drought and floods? The world's largest refugee camp, Dadaab, in Kenya, East Africa, is populated with over 500,000 Somalians whose crops failed and cattle died when the droughts came. They arrived destitute and are now stateless. Some 40 per cent of the coastal population of West Africa lives in towns threatened by rising seas. People say simply: 'We are looking for a place to go.' Climate change impacts every level of food security, energy, water supplies and health, with a ripple effect on conflict, poverty, employment and more. It risks putting back decades of development achievements.

If you enjoy TED talks take a quick look at James Balog's TED talk on extreme ice loss. Time-lapse cameras set up in the Arctic show the ice breaking up. It is truly frightening to see ice a mile deep and three miles wide vanish entirely in just 75 minutes – and that's real time. The Arctic is now a Greenpeace priority.

In 2015, classical musicians performed 'Requiem for the Arctic Ice' outside Shell's HQ in London; Shell have since announced the oil found doesn't justify the investment and their Arctic drilling has been cancelled for the 'forseeable future'. Whilst environmentalists cheer, the Arctic as we know it, referred to as 'the canary in the coalmine' for global warming, is dying even as you read this book.

It's the way you tell it

The canary is a friend of the mythical frog being gently warmed in a pan of water. It is more comfortable in the water than out, which leads, inevitably, to a dead frog. The concept that whole cities and countries could be under water by the end of this century is simply not today's main meal. What about the fuel to run our cars, the power we need to heat our homes?

In Canada, extracting bitumen from Alberta's tar sands has become the biggest industrial project worldwide. Huge open mines, pipelines and roads are replacing pristine forests and lakes, with expansion planned to cover an area the size of Florida. In the USA, meanwhile, the recent growth of fracking is hailed as a huge success – net US imports of energy have reduced by a third between 2011 and 2013 as a result.

The rest of the world is looking on, and the lure of fracking now beckons across Europe. You can imagine a struggling land-owner's thought process: *If farming doesn't support my family, I'm obviously going to consider selling mineral rights for fossil fuel exploration* ... And the immediate benefits only go sour when the water supply becomes contaminated, fish die and the family's health suffers. After all, you can't drink money and the negative impact of the mining process in the US is only now coming together as evidence. Wake up, everyone!

Even putting these arguments to one side, this is still a fossil fuel and for our future health and happiness we need to reduce our use of fossil fuels and keep them *in* the ground – not find new/better/worse ways to get them *out* of the ground.

THE RIVET POPPER HYPOTHESIS

Stanford biologists Paul and Anne Ehrlich understand communicating climate change is an issue. Back in 1981 they wrote a book, short titled *Extinction*. The preface makes the point they wished, and the Rivet Popper Hypothesis is now well-known enough to be part of university lectures. Here it is:

As you walk from the terminal to your airliner, you notice a man on a ladder busily prying rivets out of its wing. Somewhat concerned, you saunter over to the rivet-popper and ask him just what the hell he's doing.

'I work for the airline – Growthmania Intercontinental,' the man informs you, 'and the airline has discovered that it can sell these rivets for $2 apiece.'

'But how do you know you won't fatally weaken the wing doing that?' you enquire.

'Don't worry,' he assures you. 'I'm certain the manufacturer made this plane much stronger than it needs to be, so no harm's done. Besides, I've taken lots of rivets from this wing and it hasn't fallen off yet. Growthmania Airlines needs the money; if we didn't pop the rivets, Growthmania wouldn't be able to continue expanding. And I need the commission they pay me – fifty cents a rivet!'

'You must be out of your mind!'

'I told you not to worry; I know what I'm doing. As a matter of fact, I'm going to fly on this flight also, so you can see there's absolutely nothing to be concerned about.'

Any sane person would, of course, go back into the terminal, report the gibbering idiot and Growthmania Airlines to the airline regulators and make reservations with another carrier.

Rivet-popping on Spaceship Earth consists of aiding and abetting the extermination of species and populations of non-human organisms. Some of these species supply or could supply important direct benefits to humanity, and all of them are involved in providing – currently for free – public services, without which society could not persist.

Ecosystems, like well-made airplanes, tend to have redundant subsystems and other 'design' features that permit them to continue functioning after absorbing a certain amount of abuse. A dozen rivets, or a dozen species, might never be missed. On the other hand, a thirteenth rivet popped from a wing flap, or the extinction of a key species involved in the cycling of nitrogen, could lead to a serious accident.

Joining the dots

The Ehrlichs were clear. People removing the rivets of planet Earth weren't malign, just uninformed. We still have a chance to stop taking out the rivets. It will happen when we join up the dots. When we wake up to the real links – is the short-term gain of fracked gas worth the use of toxic chemicals poured into the earth to extract it and the amount of CO_2 poured into the atmosphere when we use it? How much time can we buy through short-term measures until we've developed longer-term solutions? What sort of world do we wish to live in? How many species can we wipe out before the 'level of abuse' becomes too great?

When our politicians realise we, the electorate, are serious about something being done and are 100 per cent behind them doing it, they *will* listen. So it's up to you and me. Time to refocus on creating the sort of world we wish to live in, not a pie-in-the-sky constant-economic-growth world, where people with resources trample over those without. Think of it as insurance. Even if the odds are low that my house will go up in flames, I'll insure it just in case. It doesn't cost that much to insure, but if I don't and the house burns down, there's no way I could afford another.

Leading climate-change scientist Professor Chris Rapley created and presented a piece of theatre about climate change. He called it *2071* because that is the year his eldest grandchild will be his age. In his words, 'It's not about the science, it's about the future we wish to create.' That is why he travels with his show to reach out with indisputable scientific evidence, presented in an easy-to-absorb way. The audience reacts in stunned silence. No one who's seen it puts forward counter-arguments. The job of the Intergovernmental Panel on Climate Change (IPCC) is to look at all the science and assess its validity. The findings of its latest (fifth) report were summed up by John Kerry, US secretary of state:

'It's clear that climate change is real, it's happening now, human beings are the cause of the transformation and only human beings can save the world from its worst impacts.'

Evolving to survive

So what can you and I do? Given the choice between being a frog in the simmering pot or putting aside some of our personal comforts to sustain the world, it's obvious the choice we need to make. And the more of us who focus on sustainability, the greater our influence on companies and governments.

The United Nations is supporting the development of visionary, global, 'Sustainable Development Goals', which include peaceful societies, an end to poverty, a commitment to stop climate change and to work in global partnership to achieve this. But we all know that bottom-up works best, and in the case of climate change I'm willing to bet that reducing consumer demand will work faster than top-down laws and pledges. Manufacturers give us what we want to buy. *We* have the choice. So here's what *you* can do (and you'll see there's a common theme here):

- **Buy less stuff.** Review what you actually need for yourself and your family – we need much less than we think. A lot of our spending has morphed from 'I would like to have it' to 'I need it' without really thinking it through. The three Rs are common-sense principles that everyone understands – Reduce, Re-use and Recycle.

- **Refuse to accept stuff.** Next time you order a drink, just say, 'No straw, thanks.' Millions of non-biodegradable plastic straws create massive beach litter worldwide. Better still, suggest the bar/restaurant only gives out straws when people ask for them.

- **Buy different stuff.** Did you know your toothpaste, soap and face cream is likely to be bulked up with plastic dust? Known as microbeads, they are designed to 'disappear' into the waste system – to be eaten by fish, to be eaten by us. You and I have probably eaten loads of plastic without ever knowing. Governments are working to get the stuff banned. For a quicker result, check out www.storyofstuff. org and don't buy the products.

- **Use less.** It's been pointed out that in California you never see washing drying on the line despite the sunshine. So if you can, hang your washing out, save the dryer for rainy days and feel good about using less electricity. Think twice before you use your car. Walking and cycling cost nothing/little and are incredibly good for you. And even if you commute, you might be able to walk/cycle part of the journey.

- **Go green, go local.** There is a positive, personal economic dimension to this too. The more people use renewable energy, the lower prices become. The more local, seasonal food you eat, the lower your grocery bill.

In these ways, we can all do our bit. And as well as the environmental, financial and proven health benefits to the above, there is also a positive spiritual dimension. After all, the West consumes more than the rest of the world and so its populace will have to make a proportionately greater sacrifice in relative living standards in order to take that important step towards a more equitable and generous sharing of resources in the world. But that is a good thing.

Environment, economy and population

It is not just the climate; it is the whole of our environment that is at risk. We have been brought up to acquire things on an unbelievable scale, all of which are manufactured or made using trees, crops and food growing on the Earth or minerals from within it. Absolutely everything you and I live on comes out of the ground, is grown on it or feeds off it. We are part of this system, not apart from it, and we are dependent on it, not in control. Look around the room you are in: wood in chairs, floors and beams; cotton and wool and oil-based synthetics in curtains, upholstery, clothing; clay in crockery and bricks; metal in radiators, electrics and the building's structure; stone, cork and clay in floors, concrete and cement; silicon for glass; oil for paint, plastics and to power our light and heat. Then take a moment to think about how these natural elements can be best shared between all of us living here.

Take food, for example. As Carolyn Steel wrote in her book *Hungry City*:

> *Feeding cities arguably has a greater social and physical impact on us and our planet than anything else we do. Yet few of us are conscious of the process. Food arrives on our plates as if by magic, and we rarely stop to wonder how it might have got there.*
>
> *But when you think that every day, for a city the size of London, enough food for 30 million meals must be produced, transported, sold, cooked, eaten and disposed of again, and that something similar must happen every day for every city on earth, it is remarkable that those of us living in cities get to eat at all.*

The United Nations forecasts a world population peak of 9.22 billion by 2075. That's about 47 per cent more people than were around at the beginning of the twenty-first century, and we are already at 7.3 billion in 2015. In 60 years, when your children or grandchildren are still around, there'll be one and a half times as many people to feed, clothe, house and sustain as there were fifteen years ago. Given that a billion of the 7.1 billion in today's world already struggle to find the food, water and basic health care to live a decent life, what hope is there for the 2 billion who are about to join them? How on earth (sorry) are we going to feed all these people, to say nothing of ensuring they have a roof over their heads, clean water and a life worth living? UN Sustainable Development Goals can set the framework, but it's going to be a huge challenge.

And yet governments and headlines still focus on economic growth – businesses and wages must grow to produce the sound economic environment to keep us happy. 'How will we pay for education and health care and look after the most vulnerable without decent tax revenues?' they argue. We are only just emerging from a global recession, so we know we don't want to go back there. And we're still reluctant to pay for the costs of environmental requirements ... but if there's no environment, it'll be too late for Plan B.

Remember '*oikos*', the Greek root for everything 'eco'? It means 'home' or 'household'. But it's primarily hijacked by economists these days; how come it's always the financial people we listen to, when we know money doesn't give us a life worth living? Perhaps because we *think* we can control the financial and economic systems of the world, and know that managing the interconnected natural weather systems that warm the seas and bring the rain and wind is much more difficult. Have we been hoodwinked? Are we that gullible? Climate change forecasts have a 20-year record of getting it right; something never claimed by economic modelling. We know what we need to do. We just need to move to a new level of consciousness where we proactively try to minimise our impact.

The United Nations Environment Programme got 1,400 scientists to contribute to a report which took five years to prepare, called the Global Environment Outlook. They agreed that 'human consumption has far outstripped available resources. Each person on earth now requires a third more land to supply his or her needs than the planet can supply'. No wonder the planet is stressed.

Biologist Paul Ehrlich again: 'As nature is progressively impoverished, its ability to provide a moderate climate, cleanse air and water, recycle wastes, protect crop from pests, replenish soils and so on will be increasingly degraded. The human population will be growing as the capacity of Earth to support people is shrinking ... the familiar world of today will disappear within the lifespan of many people now alive.'

Our joint consciousness is being stirred, albeit frustratingly slowly. Naomi Klein writes in *This Changes Everything* about the need for an 'alternative world view ... embedded in inter-dependence rather than hyper-individualism, reciprocity rather than dominance and cooperation rather than hierarchy'. Those living generous lives have that world view already, so let's get a few facts at our fingertips so we can spread it.

Palm oil: scourge of the rainforest

Palm oil is vegetable oil from palm trees. Though not listed in the ingredients as palm oil, it is a confirmed or suspected 'invis-ible' ingredient in 43 out of 100 of the UK's bestselling grocery brands. Look closer and it's really 43 out of 62, since the 100 bestselling brands include drinks. So what?

Palm oil is popular with manufacturers as it is the cheapest edible oil they can get. To source it, vast tracts of the indigenous forests of Indonesia and Malaysia have given way to palm oil plantations, a process that involves the loss of 90 per cent of the wildlife in those areas. Global demand means that huge swathes of African forest are now being cut for palm oil plantations. Cut means totally cleared. Without wildlife, indigenous populations cannot hunt, so human life disappears from the area as well. In order to have soaps and detergents, chocolate (especially 'choco-late-flavour') biscuits, snacks, bread and cereals, we have jointly been responsible for wiping out an area equivalent to 28 million acres so far – in Indonesia alone. It is an interesting thought that, as you munch through your breakfast cereal each morning, you could be munching through a little portion of the rainforest and voting for the extinction of the orangutan.

However much we love KitKat, Dairy Milk, Special K, Pringles and Persil, they are not worth it until they stop using palm oil and shift to sustainable vegetable oil. There is an official body looking at sustainable palm oil, but in the meantime, the more you eat and use this stuff, the more rainforest will be destroyed to grow more palm oil crops.

Rainforests and wildlife: jewels of the Earth

The Amazonian rainforest, the largest surviving rainforest on Earth, spreads over a billion acres of Brazil, Venezuela, Columbia, Ecuador and Peru. Some people have called rainforests the 'lungs of the world'. They cover 7 per cent of the world's surface and provide 20 per cent of the world's oxygen needs by continuously recycling carbon dioxide into oxygen. Free, gratis and for nothing. Just to make sure we are on the same page – *oxygen is the stuff we need to breathe*. More than half of the world's plants, animals and insects live in the tropical rainforests. A single hectare of primary rainforest (untouched by humans) has more biodiversity than can be found in the whole of North America – about 2 billion hectares' worth.

Rainforests support the livelihoods of 1.6 billion people including many indigenous tribes with unique and irreplaceable cultures. They store water, regulate rainfall and are home to thousands of medicinal plants. They act as a natural climate regulator and global cooling mechanism. They absorb, store and recycle between 10 and 15 per cent of our global carbon emissions just by being there.

Clouds created by the rainforest put 20 billion tonnes of water into the atmosphere, which falls as rain both locally and thousands of miles away. The rain feeds rivers and lakes and supports millions of people whose lives depend on it for their own needs as well as food and crops.

But the forest is disappearing. In Brazil (which has been monitoring deforestation since 1970 and includes 60 per cent of the Amazon basin) 20 per cent of the rainforest has disappeared since measuring started. The over-arching impetus is economic. There's insatiable demand for soybean, palm oil, logged wood, beef cattle and cereals to generate cash. Lack of regulation sees illegal logging run rampant. So an area the size of a football pitch disappears every four seconds. In the David and Goliath battle between indigenous peoples and agribusinesses, might is winning. Short-term gain, the ambition to grow food exports and create more immediate wealth, is exchanged for longer-term loss. And in creating demand for the goods, we are effectively destroying the ecosystem that enabled their creation.

In the Democratic Republic of Congo (DRC), Virunga, the first national park in Africa and a UNESCO World Heritage site, has been battling SOCO, a London-listed oil company hoping to drill for oil in the park. Is this more important than the preservation of the rare mountain gorillas? The local population want to keep their lifestyle and their lake for fish and fishing more than they want better roads and schools. They want to protect the gorillas and grow tourism. An Oscar-nominated film, *Virunga*, was released in 2014 and soon afterwards SOCO said they would withdraw from DRC. But under a year later, DRC's president announced he intends to negotiate with UNESCO to 'redraw the boundaries of the national park' and allow oil exploration. Almost simultaneously, the Church of England announced it would sell its 3 million SOCO shares, so pressure does work. But where is the over-arching lobby to keep fossil fuels in the ground? And why aren't more of SOCO's shareholders protesting?

If we care, we must act. When every one of us recognises our responsibilities for the stewardship of our wonderful and unique environment with its ancient cultures and treasure trove of wildlife and plants, we can put pressure on governments and commerce. If we agree that we need the rainforests with their mediating influence on climate and incredible number of 'rivets' much, much more than we need any more stuff, we mustn't sit on our hands until it's too late. Virunga National Park is on the brink of irrevocable change.

It is estimated that between 36 and 50 different species are becoming extinct every day, mainly through deforestation. At the conservative end of the scale, that's over 13,000 species every year. An awful lot of rivets. It is difficult to be more precise because biologists reckon many of the species have not yet been discovered.

If reality is at the top end of the estimate, we are destroying 18,250 species every year.

21 per cent of all known mammals,
30 per cent of all known amphibians,
12 per cent of all known birds,
35 per cent of conifers and cycads,
17 per cent of sharks,
27 per cent of reef-building corals,

assessed for the IUCN Red List of Threatened Species are threatened with extinction.

International Union for the Conservation of Nature and
Natural Resources

Not long left

'When the last tree is cut down,
The last fish eaten,
The last stream poisoned,
You will realise that you cannot eat money.'

Native American saying

In the last 100 years, 95 per cent of the world's tigers have disappeared as a result of hunting, poaching and removal of their natural habitat. Bye, bye, tiger. Such a shame there won't be any anymore ...

In the late 1980s, the amount of wild fish around the world started its steady decline due to overfishing. At the moment, the World Wildlife Fund estimates there are two or three times more fishing boats scouring the oceans than would keep fish stocks sustainable. Fish, with or without chips, could soon be a memory. We will have eaten them all ... or, at least, cleared out entire areas of the seabed into huge drag nets and chucked back the dead fish, all the while uprooting coral and plant life we can't sell. The bluefin tuna is now officially an endangered species, yet it is still being hunted down to supply our dining tables and restaurants. It is already one of the most expensive foods in the world and in Japan, where it is a delicacy, they are stockpiling deep-frozen bluefin in anticipation of rising prices come the inevitable global shortage.

Farmed fish – and incredibly, yes, they are fed fishmeal – are now increasing and there is some light at the end of the tunnel, thanks in no small measure to www.fishfight.net. Set up by chef/campaigner Hugh Fearnley-Whittingstall in 2010, successes notched up so far include 50 per cent of the EU catch *not* being chucked back to sea, UK supermarkets labelling sustainable fish, and fish-and-chip shops offering less-common varieties. Next stop: marine conservation areas. All these gains are due to people doing something incredibly simple with a big combined impact, working together in a way that makes supermarkets and politicians take note. Actor/comedian Stephen Fry is a Fish Fight supporter who summed it up nicely when he said:

'It's so fantastically easy for us to make a difference by doing a small something and so appallingly easy for us to be complicit in a complete disaster by doing a big nothing. So what's it to be then?'

So it's down to us

Fish stock *can* regenerate. The Earth *can* regenerate. We just need to give them a chance. Politicians need our votes and businesses need our money. Plain and simple. We are more influential than we think.

Around the world, online campaigning goes from strength to strength. In the UK we are very fortunate: firstly because we have established campaigning organisations like Friends of the Earth and Greenpeace; secondly, because major supermarkets compete for market share and are incredibly responsive to public feedback and views. Thanks to all those barcodes, they know on the hour what is or is not selling, to whom and where. A downturn in sales of a particular product hits the tills and profits instantly. Buy less and less will be stocked. Friend of throw less out because you've bought too much. More thought, less impulse.

We each have a simple and straightforward choice. We can carry on ignoring the science – the 'inconvenient truth' as Al Gore called it – and we can convince ourselves that our tiny contribution or lack of it won't make any difference at all. Or we can change our behaviour and watch the ripple spread to influence our children and friends. Put your hand up if you're eating less meat and fish; if someone in the family is now veggie or vegan. Look at the great YouTube clip of Luiz Antonio, still in a high chair, working out that he doesn't want to eat animals. Be one of the growing number of people who are becoming healthier and happier and putting the survival of future generations (for make no mistake, that *is* what's at stake) at the heart of our own actions.

What we can do

It is one thing to be a responsible citizen, to buy low-energy light bulbs, to turn off the lights, to insulate our lofts, to take the train not the plane, to waste less, to favour small, local producers rather than stuff flown halfway round the world ... By doing all these things we relearn how good fresh food tastes in season, save energy and often money as well. A sort of environmental win-win. We are good and get rewarded. We release that bit of us that wants to be a superhero!

It is another and much more important thing to live responsibly and be instrumental in creating the cultural shift that will help save the planet for our children, grandchildren and for future generations we will never know. This is more generous behaviour. By stretching out from our comfort zone and thinking less about convenience, special offers and low prices at any cost, we will be able to look back on our lives and know we did our bit to help others. It's a choice that's simple enough. Think before buying, read the ingredients, avoid oranges in plastic nets and plastic drinking straws, ask yourself if what you're about to do is respectful of other people, animals and the planet ... or is it helping to destroy them?

This takes us in the opposite direction from much that most of us currently take for granted. We are consumers, we have been educated to achieve and led to believe in growing GDP and a rising standard of living. And that includes the freedom to travel, to chuck away old for new, to treat clothes as disposable after a season, to eat the food we like irrespective of season, to buy quickly without thinking it through too much. But why not, instead, join the growing minority who already care? Invest a tiny bit more time and thought in focusing on what *really* creates a good and worthwhile life.

The undisputed truth is that the way we are spending our money and wasting our resources combine to place excessive and unnecessary strain on those ecosystems on which we will still be dependent in 2100 – oxygen, rain, river systems and oceans. Nature and the natural world supports absolutely every part of our lives. So turn the heating down a bit, think twice when you buy baby veg from Africa. It's not only the freight costs, it's also the carbon footprint.

It is great to support campaigning charities like Friends of the Earth, Greenpeace or WWF – and to buy Fairtrade goods. There are over 4,500 products helping provide a decent living to 1.4 million people in developing nations across the world. It's about more than bananas, sugar and coffee. Look for Fairtrade wine, cola, curry powder, olive oil, nuts, flowers, cotton … if you can't see them, change where you shop and do your bit for a more egalitarian world. Simple, generous behaviour.

The intangible things we do can have an even greater impact. Set aside a bit of time to learn about the issues and start talking them through with your friends and neighbours. Be informed enough to challenge media headlines, often placed by PR firms and vested interests. Be alert to advances in technology. Are you comfortable debating the pros and cons of renewable energy with friends who see wind and solar farms as a blight on the landscape?

Grow some of your own veg – even if it's only herbs. Serve a totally veggie or vegan meal and make it delicious – what better way to get a sustainability debate going? A huge amount of 'ignorance is bliss' still prevails and there's a very good chance you will soon be amazed at how much you have learnt while others have not had time even to think about the issues. It's just a question of priorities. When you've found out what happens to those bargain chicken pieces before they arrive sanitised and wrapped on the shelf, you may find you aren't so keen on buying them. Is the convenience of plastic netted fruit worth the death of seabirds and turtles?

If there is one thing that companies, businesses and politicians really understand and react to swiftly, it is a reduction or loss of income and support. Public opinion creates political action and change. Consumers led the challenge to supermarkets stocking unsustainably fished tuna and it worked. Supermarkets have by far the best marketing antennae in the Western world.

Politicians of every colour focus on a subject when the people they govern care and talk to them about it, in small groups and en masse. They want us to engage, not opt out. And companies spend millions on trend research to find out what we'll be buying next year – and further millions on analyses to find out what we're not buying anymore and why. If we all decided not to buy products with palm oil in, deforestation should drastically reduce. We can do this. We can make it happen.

To make it simple, here are a few initiatives that are making a difference and that are keen to get *you* involved too.

> '*If you think you are too small to make an impact, try going to bed with a mosquito.*'
>
> Dalai Lama

WeForest and Cool Earth

Trees do many wonderful things, including creating cloud cover to reflect the sun's rays. WeForest (www.weforest.org) estimates that if we can increase cloud cover by 2 per cent, global warming will be stabilised. Their approach is simple and backed by science. They reforest areas with productive forests, so it's not worthwhile for local people to get involved in logging. They plant indigenous trees that can be harvested, improve the soil and bring back biodiversity, *and* plant crops in their shade, so villagers can earn a decent living and educate their kids. WeForest have so far planted 8.5 million of the estimated 2 trillion new trees needed over the next 10 years to stabilise our climate.

Did you know 350 million people live in the rainforest? It was news to me. Cool Earth (www.coolearth.org) focuses on protecting strategically placed rainforest – land that without intervention would be cleared and that often forms a protective blockade for tens of thousands of adjacent acres. They work with local villagers in remote areas of South America and Africa, making them legal custodians of the land. It's the locals who have most to lose and who are most motivated to protect the land, and with Cool Earth's help they develop schools, clinics and sustainable jobs. If you want to add to the 50,000 strategically placed acres now protected by the local population, Cool Earth has made it easy; saving half an acre for local people to use rather than see it logged, cleared for monoculture or drilled for oil costs just £30, and of course you can 'go large' if you want.

Fish Fight

Fish Fight (www.fishfight.net), which I've already mentioned, was set up in 2010 by chef Hugh Fearnley-Whittingstall. He started with the benefit of chef celebrity status, as well as building on some public awareness of the overfishing issue which had already been created by the 2006 film *The End of the Line*. The Fish Fight story shows how much someone with Hugh's influence can do. We pay attention to celebrities, the media pay attention to celebrities, even the politicians line up behind them, and other celebrities follow their lead. Brilliant job, Hugh!

Fighting to save depleting global fish stocks, the first aim was to change EU laws which forced fishermen to throw up to 50 per cent of their edible catch back into the sea dead. The online campaign went global with 870,000 people signing up their support from all over the world. In the UK, MEPs and Westminster MPs responded to thousands of emails and tweets; across Europe celebrity chefs and climate-change activists led the charge, and after three years of lobbying, the EU voted to ban fish discards – meaning 50 per cent more fish to eat and 50 per cent less waste because *people* demanded it. *We* demanded it.

The Fish Fight TV documentaries about the campaign attracted a regular audience of 3 million, while the film went round the world and got shown at 11 international film festivals. The online audience grew to 16 million.

My daughter got the Fish Fight message so loud and clear I feel sorry for any restaurant waiter when she's thinking about eating fish. Out comes the Good Fish Guide app and then, with a smile combined with a look which says 'Don't even think about fudging your answer,' she asks: 'Can you tell me where you get your cod/bream/prawns from?' The waiter will respond with not enough information. 'No, for the cod I need to know exactly which sea area please. Are they sustainably fished?' If they can't answer one/all, she sticks to her guns and orders the veg risotto! And will probably tweet about it too.

Restaurants, fish-and-chip shops and supermarkets have all responded to more informed consumers happy to eat lesser-known, often cheaper, less-endangered fish. And now people know what the issues are, they get it. And they realise the power they generate by acting together. Thousands have lobbied for the creation of fishing-free Marine Conservation Zones in oceans around the world to allow fish stocks to recover.

If you eat fish, ask your fishmonger about its sourcing. Look for the 'Certified Sustainable Seafood' label when you're supermarket shopping. Only buy tinned tuna which is labelled 'pole and line caught'. Help keep fish on the menu.

Solar Schools

Schools have large roofs ... perfect for generating solar power. If you haven't heard of Solar Schools (www.solarschools.org.uk)

already, it's probably because – although it's an award-winning brainchild of environmental charity 10:10 – there's a limit to their capacity to manage growth. 10:10's vision is that people power works even when policies stall, so they advise schools to set realistic fundraising targets for their very own solar roof and everyone chips in to make it happen. Just think: 30,000 school roofs would create a *serious* amount of clean energy and reduce their overheads.

As ever, some of the best ideas work because they're so obvious. Join the school PTA and you will be organising the next summer fête to drum up funds for school 'extras', so why not tackle something more strategic like arranging for the school to generate electricity that doesn't rely on the main grid?

At the heart of the Solar Schools programme is the idea of getting everyone involved – kids, parents, the local community – and crowdfunding. What better way to teach children about climate change, energy, project management and teamwork?

No Net Loss

The concept of No Net Loss has been around for some time. It works like this. If I clear a forest, drain some wetlands, clear a construction site or mine for minerals, I do my best to avoid doing harm to the greatest extent I can, but when, inevitably, I damage the ecosystem, then I agree to do something that will compensate for it. Generosity to the environment if you like: no damage or, in an ideal world, a net positive impact. Where I take something away, I enable it to be recreated elsewhere.

Is this an impossible dream? The battles between oil companies and indigenous people suffering the impact of oil spills and contaminated water have been going on for years. Growing economies are using more water and more energy rather than less. It's a challenge to believe that your individual action will count. So think of it in terms of leading a cultural shift to one where the planet matters as much as people. Add your voice to the online protest petition. Email those elected to create a better life for all.

For climate change, No Net Loss means avoiding energy use as much as possible, using all our energy efficiently and offsetting the climate impacts of the energy used. Every little thing you do in this direction helps shift the norms as well as reducing your personal energy consumption.

For biodiversity, it means keeping fossil fuels in the ground, and pushing mining, utility, forestry, agriculture and tourism companies to adopt No Net Loss/positive impact policies. Some leading global conglomerates have already done so and the pressure is growing on those dragging their heels.

The next step is to bring the concept of No Net Loss into our everyday lives – think No Net Loss labelling. Together with sustainable sourcing and Fairtrade, we will be able to incorporate a No Net Loss Kitemark. Manufacturers will guarantee that all components are from sustainable sources. There will be an audit trail to ensure environmental damage is minimised, residual harm compensated for and communities enhanced rather than destroyed in the process. We will go shopping and look for the No Net Loss label on tuna, coffee, bread, jeans, computers, mobile phones and more.

Even before this happens, we can all take part in the process now. We need to check where the products we buy come from and, for example, whether a particular brand of biscuit includes the globally ruinous palm oil as an ingredient. There are 30 different ways of describing palm oil just to make it difficult, but if you mean business check out the words online (www.palmoilinvestigations.org) and if the answer is 'yes', stop buying it unless it has a 'sustainable palm oil' badge. If the answer is 'no', tell your friends, blog, tweet, spread the word. Nothing is as contagious as word of mouth combined with an impact on sales.

Ecocide: legislation to protect the planet

Ecocide brings the idea of No Net Loss into international law.

There are four global Crimes Against Peace enshrined in international law by the United Nations. They cover genocide, slavery, torture, massacre and apartheid as crimes against humanity. It's these laws that hold people to account as war criminals for acts where sustained and deliberate action has been condoned by governments.

So what is ecocide? The draft law first presented to the United Nations in 2010 proposes to make 'extensive damage to, destruction of or loss of ecosystems' a crime: the fifth global Crime Against Peace. When ecocide is acknowledged as a crime in international law, those who cause damage to the planet can be held to account. Ecocide puts protection of the planet on an equal footing to the protection of people and, importantly, includes a legal duty of care for people at risk of being harmed by damage to the environment, however caused. For the first time, it would be possible to hold leaders of governments and companies personally to account to pre-empt harmful activities such as the destruction of the rainforests or mining activities that devastate landscapes. It would extend to cover natural catastrophes. For example, with ecocide on the statute books, there would be a collective 'duty of care' to nations at risk of drowning under rising sea levels. (If you're thinking of holidaying in the Maldives, go quickly ... The Maldives are just 1.3 metres above sea level; the Seychelles even less at just 1 metre. Better still, surf in Cornwall and reduce your carbon footprint.)

The idea of putting crime against the environment into international law isn't new. It was first proposed in the 1970s. So what happened? Why has it taken so long? Academics have trawled through the records to find out and their report mentions 'unilateral decisions' being made and the relevant Article being removed 'completely and somewhat mysteriously'. Am I a cynic to attribute its disappearance to vested interests and the power of lobbying?

Surely the time has come to join up our thinking and ensure some duty of care for the 1.3 million people whose island homes are in real danger of sinking under the waves. And also for the 156 million people living on and around the Bangladeshi delta, where the land is already so waterlogged that floating rafts are being used to farm.

Transition Towns

Think, act, do local. Harness the talent and power in your local community to create the place you want it to be; get together to buy from local businesses, create local energy and change things a town at a time. If almost everyone relies on the supermarkets for their shopping and national energy suppliers for their gas and electricity, there's little benefit to the local economy. Time for change.

Although triggered by concern about climate change and peak oil, the Transition Town culture and ethos is optimism. It's not about being worthy, or even green, but looking at what you've got and how to make it better. In Topsham, Devon, they asked: 'What is it that unites people in this town? Is it peak oil, or is it beer?' and then set up a brewery.

The Transition Town movement (mentioned in Chapter 8) has taken off since first starting in Totnes, Devon in 2006.

Over 3,000 people are now involved out of Totnes's total population of 8,500. At the last count, 240 UK towns and boroughs had signed up and the idea of Transition Towns has spread worldwide from Alaska to Australia, Chile to Japan. The logic is that governments are by nature short term. They need to deliver before the next election comes round so the longer-term fundamental issues slip way down the list of priorities. It's madness to suggest any elected representatives can create change in the same way as a committed group of people living in a community with a myriad of experience and passion to make their town better, accountable only to themselves with the freedom to experiment along the way. Why do it? One perspective: 'If I want something done, I know a person who knows a person, who knows a person who can get it done.'

There's no prescription. Solutions are initiated by the community. Totnes made headlines when the community rallied to keep a major coffee chain out of town. They value their independent shops more than the idea of becoming a 'clone town with clone shops'. Rob Hopkins, one of the founders, describes the movement as being like a huge open-source research-and-development project. 'Different groups try different ideas and, if the idea works, it spreads.' Like community-owned power stations and food hubs (grow your own food and sell it). And by doing stuff, Transition Towns are building the case for national change. The Fife Diet is simply about eating local food. It's been going for five years and is now the largest local food project in Europe – the carbon footprint of members of the Fife Diet is 40–60 per cent lower than the UK average. The power of lots of people making small changes to their lives and reconnecting with a healthier way of living.

Develop your Generous Gene

The environmental bandwagon is gaining momentum. You will no longer be branded a nutter when you suggest sharing your car, buying second-hand or recycling through Freecycle or eBay – my neighbour recently sold on her fitted kitchen before installing a new one. Hundreds of thousands of people are joining online groups bringing pressure to bear on businesses using environmentally dangerous ingredients in their products, and more hundreds of thousands are joining initiatives like Zero Waste Week: pledge for just a week to cut down on your waste as much as possible, recycle and reuse.

Become properly informed. Follow organisations running campaigns like Keep It In the Ground (www.theguardian. com/environment/series/keep-it-in-the-ground), Global Citizen (www.globalcitizen.org), Friends of the Earth (www.foe. co.uk), Greenpeace (www.greenpeace.org.uk) and the Ocean Conservancy (www.oceanconservancy.org). Add your name to lobby for change.

Do no harm. Start a personal No Net Loss programme. Make a conscious effort to avoid companies and products that harm our environment for the pursuit of profit. Join the growing band of people taking a stand.

Lend and share. When did you last use your electric drill, surfboard, exercise bike or sewing machine? Lending any of these little-used items out is easy and generous with www.shareable. net and www.streetbank.com.

Dump less. Avoid excess packaging, including anything with packaging you know you'll chuck straight in the bin (packaged fruit and veg, especially oranges in plastic netting). Recycle everything you possibly can. Glass is made from sand and can be recycled ad infinitum. Not recycled, it will clog up landfill sites for 'up to a million years'. An improvement on the current 50 per cent recycled can't be that difficult.

Don't waste water. Getting clean water to your tap uses lots of energy; heating it then uses more. Just because it flows, doesn't mean it's OK to keep the tap running. Watering plants with soapy dish-water from time to time is fine. Waiting till the dishwasher and washing machine have full loads before putting them on makes absolute sense. If you are still buying bottled water, give yourself a sharp slap. You have been had by peer pressure and the marketing people!

Offset your emissions. However green or well-intentioned, we all use energy and produce carbon emissions when driving, switching on the heating or heading off on holiday. So pay for (offset) your carbon emissions by making a contribution to a carbon-reducing environmental charity or project; plant a tree or help save the rainforest. If you're feeling courageous, check out your day-to-day carbon footprint on www.carbonfootprint.com and work out what you can do to reduce it. Then do it.

And reduce them. By following in the steps of the Fife Diet and aiming for 80 per cent locally sourced food you will make an enormous dent in your own carbon footprint. You don't have to give up oranges and lemons, you'll reconnect with the seasons and slow down a bit.

Conclusion

Developing Our Generous Gene

I started this book to share what I've discovered through the very personal lens that has been my life. But what is one man's view? So I've augmented it with stories from people who've inspired me and books written by others far cleverer, all the while trying to keep it simple.

If I can influence people who read it, I will be happy. A small contribution to add to thousands of others who know society needs to change and to the people already changing it. What I've discovered for myself is supported by a huge weight of evidence. If we want to be happy, we should be generous and kind to our fellow men. If we care about the future of the planet we need to take only our share and no more. Community and collaboration are the tools we need to work with, rather than competition, which only creates inequality. When we trust someone by being open and honest we can support each other. There is good in all of us and we just need to make a choice.

We can and should take control of our own destinies because we will do it quicker and quite probably better than is possible for those who govern us. We can challenge by our actions as much as our words. Communities are at the heart of change, free to innovate and experiment because it feels right. We can get there by trial and error. Communities know everything in their environment is interconnected; they don't need to think in silos; they have

the flexibility to join up the dots. As the pace of change acceler-
ates, it becomes increasingly difficult for our bureaucratic systems
to keep up. They are biased towards scale and models that wish to
predict results with a certainty that probably never existed.

This is not a 'self-help' book but a 'help others' book. I want
to encourage every reader to do something differently. To find a
little bit more time in your busy life to be generous and become
happier. Mindfulness in action. And the twist, of course, is that by
helping others you will be giving meaning to your own life. You
don't have to be in any way brainy or successful. This is an open
invitation. You can be a change-maker by example, helping create
a twenty-first-century world where society has changed so that
people are valued for who they are more than for what they have.

It's great that Pope Francis is using his influence to lead by
example, sharing his 'Ten Secrets for Happiness. Here are the
headlines:

1. Live and let live
2. Be giving of yourself to others
3. Proceed calmly in life
4. Have a healthy sense of leisure; play with your children
5. Sunday is for family; it should be a holiday
6. Create dignified jobs for young people
7. Respect and take care of nature
8. Stop being negative
9. Don't proselytise; respect others' beliefs
10. Work for peace

Not much to argue with there. So the only thing left to do now is
act. From the lists in the book, think of something *you'd* like to
do – and can. Then, rather than put it off, commit to paper your

'to do' list, or whatever it is that for you will make it happen. Pause to focus on some of the generous things people have done for you recently and jot them down: the people you admire for their generosity; the generous acts you have witnessed. Rebuff any 'don't have the time/money/ inclination' negative thoughts. Start to rewire your brain to focus on what makes you happy. Recognise that you can choose to do things differently and it could be the best decision ever! Focus on maximising your life, not your income.

If you're a joiner, there are movements to join wherever you look. If you're a go-getter, get out there and make a difference. Together, we can change the world.

To set you on your way, here's a story from Claire, a friend kind enough to read the book in draft:

'What do you do when you are not being dynamic?'

CLAIRE'S STORY

When I first met Mike, he asked me, 'What do you do when you are not being dynamic?' It really got me thinking. What *do* I do with my life other than work and look after my family? What do I do to help others?

As a result, I signed up to do a charity cycle ride, which involved cycling with 30 different people for 30 days. One of my cycles was around Hyde Park on a Boris bike with Mike! I raised money for charity, and also realised how great it felt to help other people. Also, talking to my cycle buddies over the 30 days, I realised that actually everyone wants to help someone. Everyone has a heart for generosity.

Since then, I've been completely taken aback by the reaction you get from someone when you do a random act of kindness. I bought a new pair of shoes recently, and when I came out of the shop I saw a man begging for money. I gave him enough money for a good lunch, and it felt so much more rewarding than my new shoes!

I will give the last word to Olly, founder of Shivia, in this email she sent me after reading the book:

'I thought you'd like to hear how the manuscript helped me. The morning after reading it, I was heading to work and into Caffè Nero for my usual daily caffeine kick. I passed a man huddled in his sleeping bag in a storefront, and as I was ordering my regular 'skinny Americano' I thought of what I had read the night before and changed the order. 'Actually, can you make that two coffees, please?'

On the way out, I went up to the man and handed him a coffee. He looked at first astonished, then slightly baffled and finally realised that it was for him. He smiled and said, 'Thank you, love. Appreciated.' I walked to the bus stop with a bounce in my step; today was going to be a good day.'

And my final message to you is that we all have the power to make today a good day. So start today. Soon, you will find that it's not just today you're changing. Soon, tomorrow – all our tomorrows – will be good days too.

If you've time to share your story with me, I'd accept it as a generous gesture and as an encouragement to do more to cultivate *my* Generous Gene. You can contact me here:

mike@ourgenerousgene.com
www.ourgenerousgene.com
facebook.com/ourgenerousgene
Twitter.com/ourgenerousgene
#@generousgene

Resources

'He who asks a question is a fool for a minute;
he who does not remains a fool forever.'

Chinese proverb

I f you're inspired to learn a bit more about how to maximise
your happy, generous life, this a quick overview of some of
the books, articles and websites that inspired, informed and,
yes, even changed me, whilst I was writing this book. Particular
favourites are marked with a **.

Many of the individuals mentioned have given TED talks –
so do look them up, plus of course their own websites. TED
(**www.ted.com**) was set up to share 'Ideas worth spreading'. A
huge range of clever, inspiring and funny talks by extraordinary people are available online. Everyday brain food on your
laptop or smartphone.

Introduction

Whizz-Kidz. You too can make a life-changing difference to one
young person's life by providing them with the mobility we all
take for granted. **www.whizz-kidz.org.uk**

Rainmaker Foundation. What Mike did next! A wonderful
and powerful community of people committed to 'creating a
world in which what matters most is what we do for others'.
www.rainmakerfoundation.org

1. Growing Your Generous Gene

Charles Darwin, *On the Origin of Species by Means of Natural Selection*, was first published in 1859. Darwin didn't have the benefit of today's science and based his evolutionary theory on his observations of the physical adaptations in animals, birds and plants.

Richard Dawkins, *The Selfish Gene*, uses much more science to explain his evolutionary theory, suggesting altruism happens because of the genetic connection of blood relations. Even though he concludes altruism isn't natural to human beings, he hopes we can develop a culture where we think more altruistically. I would love to emulate his million+ sales with *Our Generous Gene* – it seems more on message!

Professor Walter Goldschmidt, *The Bridge to Humanity* introduces the new idea that we are products of our environment and so able to intervene in our own evolution and development. As an optimist it's good to know that more and more neuroscientists are coming to the same conclusion.

Jeremy Rifkin, *The Empathic Civilization* develops the evolutionary debate further, looking at the very profound ways empathy has shaped our development. His ideas are explained in a great short animation, 10 minutes long. **www.youtube.com/watch?v=l7AWnfFRc7g**

Life Vest Inside, kindness keeps the world afloat. The power of the ripple effect just one person can create, changing our environment by spreading kindness. Inspirational. Useful resources and things to do. **www.lifevestinside.com**

E. F. Schumacher, *Small Is Beautiful: A Study of Economics as if People Mattered*. A collection of essays by a British economist. *The Times Literary Supplement* ranked it amongst the 100 most influential books published since the Second World War. Great book that does exactly what it says on the tin.

Pope Francis. This is the link to the full text of his 2015 encyclical Laudato Si. **www.laudatosi.com**

** **Erich Fromm,** *To Have or To Be?* is short and powerful. Fromm argues that we have a choice between a life based on self-ishness and greed or based on love, solidarity and creativity. First published in 1975 and totally relevant today.

2. Living Generously

Riane Eislers' TEDx talk on building a caring economy deserves a wider audience. I urge you to watch it. **www.youtube.com/ watch?v=f9cMcTWWDkU**

B Corps is looking for companies that want to be the best in the world and do the best for the world. A stringent certification process operates, but that's all to the good if we want to redefine success in business. **www.bcorporation.net**

SumofUs uses the power of lobbying to put pressure on unethical business practices. **www.sumofus.org**

Franklin Scholars operates a self-sustaining model. I reckon it should operate in every school in every country round the world. Why not? **www.franklinsholars.org**

Dr Richard Davidson is Professor of Psychology and Psychiatry at the University of Wisconsin-Madison. Best known for his signifi-cant research into the impact of emotions, especially meditation, on the physical make-up of the brain. Named one of the hundred most influential people in the world by *Time* magazine in 2006. **www.richardjdavidson.com**

Archbishop Desmond Tutu and Reverend Mpho Tutu, *The Book of Forgiving*. A very remarkable man and his remarkable daughter have written a simple book about how to give and receive the forgiveness that will make us whole.

4. The Secrets of Happiness

Lord Richard Layard, *Happiness: lessons from a new science*. An economist who has joined up the dots between psychology neuro-science, economics, sociology and philosophy in his research into happiness. No better source for a 'how to be happy' book.

James Maskells' TEDx talk 'Building Healthcare from Scratch' is on YouTube and an easy way to access his thinking.

Paul Zak, *The Moral Molecule* summarises his research into the feel-good hormone oxytocin and its impact on our behaviours. He's also done a TED talk worth watching.

Dan Pink, *Drive: The Surprising Trust about What Motivates Us*. He interviewed leading experts across a whole range of fields economics, psychology, survey analysis, national statistics, health, public policy – to describe how measurements of well-being can be used effectively to assess the progress of nations. **www.danpink.com**

Action for Happiness. The vision of Lord Layard, and run by the remarkable Mark Williamson, who left a successful city career to spread the why and the how. You can learn to be happier and there's a good course on offer. **www.actionforhappiness.org**

Martin Seligman, *Authentic Happiness*. If you want to be happy be generous. If you want to learn about happiness read Seligman.

Sonja Lyubomirsky, *The How of Happiness: Simple ways to lead a happier life*.

**Richard Schoch,*The Secrets of Happiness: Three Thousand Years of Searching for the Good Life.* One of my favourites!

**Viktor Frankl, *Man's Search for Meaning.* One of the most inspiring books on 'the purpose of life' ever written – a source for most self-help gurus.

Stephen Covey and Roger and Rebecca Merrill, *First Things First.* 'The most important thing is to keep the most important thing, the most important thing'. Must remember that.

John Sweeney. A lovely persuasive Irishman who created Suspended Coffees and GenKind24 ... and went on to become a chum! Get to know John and his work on the Suspended Coffees Facebook page.

5. What Is Enough?

**Charles Handy, *The Elephant and the Flea.* Another hero, great company, wise and wonderful. Credited with creating the concept of a Portfolio Life.

Oliver James, *Affluenza.* A really sensible observation, though the book could be shorter. From the same man who gave us *They F*** You Up: How to Survive Family Life* and controversial parenting advice in *How Not to F*** Them Up.* Interesting, relevant, thoughtful writer.

John Naish, *Enough: Breaking Free from the World of More.* Well written and thought provoking.

Tristram Stuart, *Waste: Uncovering the Global Food Scandal.* Truly sobering and scarcely believable; this was one of the parts of my research that truly shocked me. **www.tristramstuart.co.uk

Leo Tolstoy, *'How Much Land Does a Man Need?'* One of his most famous short stories, a parable about greed.

Freecycle. The good news is that it works. The bad news is, if you sign up, you need to be prepared for a deluge of emails. www.freecycle.org

The Giving Pledge is a commitment by the world's wealthiest individuals and families to dedicate the majority of their wealth to philanthropy. www.givingpledge.org

Akshaya Patra. A completely brilliant NGO which feeds over 1.4 million children with wholesome food in 10,845 schools across 10 states in India. Every day, for a year. For £7.50 each child. www.akshayapatra.org

Story of Stuff. Started by Annie Leonard, with a clever much-visited YouTube video of the same name, in 2007. Trailblazing behaviour. www.storyofstuff.org

Stuart Murray, *Beyond Tithing*. An intelligent book about the pros and cons of tithing. One of the cons being that people who give away 10 per cent of their income think they've done enough.

6. Poverty in Britain

Age UK. The charity formed when Age Concern and Help the Aged merged. www.ageuk.org.uk

Trussell Trust is the largest of the foodbank providers. Started in 1997, the service is efficient and always in need of volunteers. www.trusselltrust.org

Citizens Advice. With offices all over the country, CA deals constantly with the poor and the scared. If you don't think poverty exists in this country, pop into one of their centres and speak to their volunteers. www.citizensadvice.org.uk

Fareshare. A 'community food network', distributing surplus from the food industry to people who need it. www.fareshare.org.uk

The Poverty and Social Exclusion Site. A great source of reliable statistics and facts about poverty in this country. **www.poverty.ac.uk

Unicef, *Report Card 12, Children in the Developed World.* An international report that should make us all hang our heads in shame. **www.unicef.org.uk/publications/pdf/rc12-eng-web.pdf**

Save the Children UK's report into child poverty was published in May 2014, *A Fair Start for Every Child.* Downloadable. **www.savethechildren.org.uk/resources/online-library/fair-start-every-child**

7. Generosity at Home

Max De Pree, *Leadership is an Art.* The former CEO of Herman Miller who believed in creating a caring business environment first and foremost, writes simply about leadership from his personal experience. A book that has influenced people working in politics and academia as well as business.

The Parable of the Good Samaritan. Gospel of Luke, chapter 10, verses 25–37. Powerful wisdom from 2,000 years ago.

Samaritans. People who listen: an emotional support service for anyone in the UK and Ireland. **www.samaritans.org**

8. Generous Communities

The Transition Town Movement has taken off, and as with all great local initiatives, is inspiring people around the world to make wherever they live a better, stronger, healthier community **www.transitionnetwork.org**

Charity Commission. The body that oversees charities in England and Wales. Scotland and Northern Ireland have their own regulatory bodies. If you are interested in finding out about a particular charity, this is a good place to begin. If you want to cut to the chase the annual reports are as good a place as any to start. England/Wales: **www.charity-commission.gov.uk**; Scotland: **www.oscr.org.uk**; Northern Ireland: **www.charity-commissionni.org.uk**

Office for National Statistics. A good source of up-to-date figures on the state of the nation. **www.ons.gov.uk

Volunteering. Organisations with databases to match what you want to do with charities who want and need your skills: **www.do-it.org.uk**; **www.volunteering.org.uk**; **www.reachskills.org.uk**; **www.pilotlight.org.uk**

** Jonathan Sacks, *The Politics of Hope*. A wise man making a plea for a society where we collaborate more and legislate less.

Incredible Edibles. The whole inspiring point about Todmorden (as well as the Transition Town movement) is that it's a 'do it and see what happens' way of changing your part of the world, rooted in the generous sharing of food. **www.incredible-edible-todmorden.co.uk**

38 Degrees is evidence that people do really care about issues. It provides a unique route through to our policy makers and politicians and is changing the way our bureaucracy works. **www.38degrees.org.uk**

9. World Poverty

Paul Collier, *The Bottom Billio: Why the Poorest Countries Are Failing and What Can Be Done About It*. A powerful, well-written book outlining the links between war and poverty, the challenges of development agencies and questionable performance of governments. See also his *The Plundered Planet: How to Reconcile Prosperity with Nature.*

Jeffrey Sachs, *The End of Poverty: How We Can Make It Happen in Our Lifetime.* Jeffrey Sachs, Director of The Earth Institute, argues convincingly that the world's problems are solvable. **www. earth.columbia.edu**

Peter Singer, *The Life You Can Save: How to Play Your Part in Ending World Poverty.* An Australian philosopher who argues that we can end world poverty and urges us to get on with it. Clear and straightforward arguments. Singer has also written about animal liberation.

Hilde Back Education Fund works to fund the brightest future leaders of Kenya, who might otherwise never make it through lack of education. Inspiring and effective. **www.hildebackeducationfund.com**

The United Nations Refugee Agency regularly updates the facts on global refugees. No doubt my figures will be out of date by the time you read this so if you want an update consult the website. **www.unhcr.org**

A Glimmer of Hope. If you are going to Ethiopia, or even if you are not, go and help them. They have also set up a UK charity helping young people. **www.aglimmerofhope.org**

Michael Norton, *365 Ways to Change the World.* The author is the creator of numerous NGOs, a one-man ideas factory and charming with it! Good ideas at **365Ways.blogspot.co.uk**

The Orchid Project to end female genital cutting (parents love their daughters, they don't accept they mutilate them) has not won the battle yet. **www.orchidproject.org**

The Grameen Foundation uses the analogy of poor people being a bit like bonsai trees. With no space to develop, a bonsai's growth is stunted. It's the environment rather than the tree that's the issue. Their **Bankers Without Borders** scheme is a great way to get involved. **www.grameenfoundation.org**

Kiva. Investing in helping some of the world's poorest and reinvest when you get your loan back. **www.kiva.org**

Shivia. You can't get more grass-roots and high impact than Shivia's work. Operated locally in West Bengal, funded from the UK. **www.shivia.com**

Discover smaller projects looking for money and support: **www.justgiving.com; www.globalgiving.co.uk; www.givewell.org; www.thefundingnetwork.org.uk**

10. An Earth to Inherit

Keep It in the Ground. What's so great about this is that it's being run by media-savvy, professional *Guardian* journalists linked in to decision makers as much as the public. And it's making huge headway, quickly. Proof of the positive power of the media. **www.theguardian.com/environment/series/keep-it-in-the-ground**

Extreme Ice Survey. The brainchild of James Balog a remarkable man doing remarkable work. **www.extremeicesurvey.org**

Lester Brown: *Plan B 4.0. Mobilizing to Save Civilization.* How to save the world, by the director of the Earth Policy Institute; read and learn. The book is available as a free download from their website. **www.earth-policy.org**

Jonathan Safran Foer, *Eating Animals.* Exploring a subject we'd rather not look at too closely, Foer makes a powerful case for becoming a vegetarian with his depictions of factory farms and their truly degrading conditions. And then there is the impact of eating meat on the environment. **www.eatinganimals.com

Felicity Lawrence, *Not on the Label: What Really Goes Into the Food on Your Plate.* Not so much the ingredients, as the exploitation and damage to the planet. If you were to stop and think about it, you probably would not eat much of what you do, so be warned – this may change your shopping habits forever.

Carolyn Steel, *Hungry City.* How much food it takes to feed a city; never mind every city. **www.hungrycitybook.co.uk**

10:10 Remarkable 'can do' organisation that has revolutionised the communication about the challenges to our environment. **www.1010uk.org

Friends of the Earth. Environmental campaign group active in the UK and worldwide. Their website is a rich source of articles on climate change, the rainforest, palm oil and more. **www.foe.co.uk**

Greenpeace. Worldwide campaigning organisation whose website has vast amounts of information about the issues facing the planet, including palm oil, fishing and the rainforest. **www.greenpeace.org.uk**

Livestock's Long Shadow. Jointly published by LEAD (Livestock, Environment and Development) and the FAO (the UN Food and Agriculture Organization), this is a sobering take on a little-known contributor to our environmental challenges. Download it from the FAO website. **www.fao.org**

No Net Loss. The Business and Biodiversity Offsets Programme (BBOP) is a high-level group working with governments and business on the principles of no net loss or, better still, net positive impact. **bbop.forest-trends.org**

The Author

Hugely respected and experienced within the charitable sector, Mike is the founder of the **Rainmaker Foundation,** an exceptional community of individuals who are committed to making the world a better place for all. Rainmakers use their collective resources, funds, contacts and expertise to help charities and drive greater social impact.

Mike also co-founded the successful children's charity **Whizz-Kidz,** which provides mobility equipment and advice for disabled children. In the last 25 years the charity has raised over £100 million and helped more than 20,000 children and young people.

Mike personally advises numerous philanthropists and businesses on their charitable giving and how to give money away effectively.

As a speaker his inspirational stories, including being goaded into running the London Marathon during a Christmas party, have influenced many others to acts of generosity that are both life changing *and* make a real difference to the lives of others.

Mike is married with two children and lives in West London. He has run six marathons, led several charity treks and recently completed a 100-mile cycle road race. Just.

Previous books include *The More You Give The More You Get* and *Please Take One Step.*

www.ourgenerousgene.com

www.rainmakerfoundation.org

www.whizz-kidz.org.uk